AMERICAN WOMEN WRITERS

GARLAND REFERENCE LIBRARY
OF THE HUMANITIES
(VOL. 86)

AMERICAN WOMEN WRITERS
An Annotated Bibliography of Criticism

Barbara A. White

GARLAND PUBLISHING, INC. • NEW YORK & LONDON
1977

Library of Congress Cataloging in Publication Data

White, Barbara Anne.
  American women writers.

  (Garland reference library of the humanities ; v. 86)
  Includes index.
    1. American literature--Women authors--History and
criticism--Bibliography. I. Title.
Z1229.W8W45   [PS147]   016.81'09'9287   76-52677
ISBN 0-8240-9887-0

Z1229
W8
W45

To my grandmother, Martha Jones Busacker, and the memory of my grandfather, John Busacker

CONTENTS

PREFACE

Since the beginning of the new feminist movement in the late
1960's, women's studies courses have become numerous in our
colleges and universities, and they have been accompanied by a
significant amount of scholarly and critical work on women.
Almost every teacher and scholar involved has had occasion to
note the lack of bibliographic control in the area of women's
studies; we have had to spend much of our time trying to
uncover both primary and secondary materials.

   In the field of literature, where there has been a resurgence of
interest in women writers, the first bibliographic task was to
identify the works of "lost" or forgotten women and the less well-
known writings of famous women. Thus the first of the published
bibliographies which deal specifically with women and American
literature, *Women and Literature: An Annotated Bibliography of
Women Writers* (Cambridge, Mass.: Cambridge-Goddard
Graduate School, 1972), emphasized primary materials, the prose
fiction of individual women writers. Now, when feminist critics
and teachers have become familiar with much of this literature, it
is possible to turn our attention to a second important
undertaking—providing access to the secondary material, the
criticism on women writers. Carol Fairbanks Myers' *Women in
Literature: Criticism of the Seventies* (Metuchen, N.J.: Scarecrow
Press, 1976) is a step in this direction. It is a bibliography of
criticism written from 1970 to 1975 on women writers and female
characters in literature. Although there is a section on
background works for the study of women in literature, most of
the entries are arranged in an alphabetical list of individual
writers. The bibliography is thus a useful tool for finding
criticism on particular women writers.

   But what about women writers in general? As feminist critics
have been discovering or reinterpreting the works of specific

writers, they have also been asking broad questions: Do women writers portray common experiences? What have their lives been like? What problems have they faced in writing? What contributions have they made to literature? Is there any identifiable female point of view, or subject matter, or style? Feminist students, teachers, librarians, scholars, and critics need access to the answers which have thus far been provided to these questions—in other words, we need a bibliography of criticism on women writers in general. "Criticism on women writers in general" can be construed in different ways, but I have taken it to mean criticism which treats three or more individual writers or comments on women writers as a distinct group. The ideal bibliography of this criticism, as I see it, would be a reasonably comprehensive annotated listing of works on women writers of all nationalities, in all genres, from the time women first began to write until the present. Needless to say, this is a vast undertaking and must be the work of more than one person.

My contribution is limited to published criticism on American women writers of fiction, poetry, and drama, though of course many items I list deal with both American and English writers or specify no nationality. Except in a few cases, where British publications deal specifically with American writers or have heavily influenced American criticism, the criticism included originated in America. I have also limited the material to be included in other ways. The restriction to American writers limits the time period; the coverage extends through 1975, although I have added items published in 1976 and 1977 as they have come to my attention. In regard to form, articles in newspapers (except for the magazine sections) and dissertations are excluded; dissertations can easily be found in *Dissertation Abstracts* and James Woodress's *Dissertations in American Literature*. Reviews which treat several books by women are included if they make generalizations about writing by women; if a reviewer merely discusses each book separately, the review is excluded. The same principle is followed in the case of introductions to anthologies and interviews with writers.

In speaking above of the "ideal" bibliography of criticism on women writers, I said it should be "reasonably comprehensive," and I have followed this goal in my bibliography. The difficulties in compiling a bibliography which could be called "definitive" are very great. One has only to recall Virginia Woolf doing research for *A Room of One's Own* in the British Museum, Virginia Woolf overwhelmed by the vast number of books on women written by "agreeable essayists, light-fingered novelists, young men who have taken the M. A. degree; men who have taken no degree; men who have no apparent qualification save that they are not women" (*A Room of One's Own*, Ch. II). It is not unlikely that the writer of a treatise on bicycles, let us say, will digress for a few pages to give us his opinion of the "lady novelists." There is also the problem that critics as well as novelists have been ridiculed for writing specifically about women and have sometimes disguised their topic. Books of criticism in the 1970's are likely to be given titles like *The Female Imagination* or *Women and Literature*, but it is not easy to guess that *The Novel and Society* is a study of women writers. For several such reasons the indexing of criticism on women writers has not been particularly thorough or impressive. I suspect I have omitted some relevant items from this bibliography and welcome any additions.

The categories established for this bibliography are:

I. *Biography.* Works which are mainly biographical, although they may describe the writers' works and provide some criticism. Covers interviews and accounts of personal acquaintance with writers.

II. *Special Groups.* Criticism on a specific group of female authors. Covers minority group women, lesbians, and writers from a particular section of the country.

III. *Special Topics.* Criticism which deals with a particular genre or theme in the work of women writers.

IV. *Literary History.* Survey of women's literature in the past. Includes discussions of the general contributions women have made to literature.

V. *Contemporary Assessments.* Appraisals and descriptions of literature by women who are the critics' contemporaries.
VI. *Feminine Sensibility.* Works on the question of whether women and men write differently, whether there is an identifiable female style, sensibility, or tradition in literature.
VII. *Problems.* Material on the problems women writers have faced because of their gender.
VIII. *Phallic Criticism.* (The term is from Mary Ellmann's *Thinking about Women.* See No. 327.) Studies of critics' and publishers' discriminatory treatment of female writers.
IX. *Feminist Literary Criticism.* Works on the definition, philosophy, and approaches of the new feminist criticism.
X. *Miscellaneous.* Accounts of women's motives and methods in writing; advice and admonition; anthologies and periodical issues on women writers; a few items which do not fit the other categories.

These categories are for the reader's convenience in browsing; obviously many critical works fit into more than one classification. I do not list any item more than once, but at the end of each category I list the numbers of relevant items which have been placed in other categories. An additional reference aid is the index to critics and editors.

I have checked and annotated all entries. In preparing the entries, my main concern has been to describe the content of a work, rather than its physical characteristics; thus collation statements are not detailed. Nor have I attempted to list every single appearance of a work. The intent in both cases is to provide enough information for easy access. "Discussion" refers to letters to the editor or reader reactions in sections designated for that purpose; discussion is annotated only when it seems particularly significant.

I am grateful to the following people for their assistance: Juan Freudenthal, who encouraged the project in its initial stages; Jane Block, Rachel Helm, and Mel Regnell of the University of New Hampshire Library staff, who made special efforts to obtain materials for me; and Harvey Epstein, who patiently proofread and offered helpful advice and support.

Durham, New Hampshire   B.A.W.
April, 1977

INTRODUCTION

In one sense this bibliography needs no further introduction. The annotations provide a quick overview of the topic. For the reader who is unfamiliar with criticism on women writers as a group, the titles alone are revealing: Do Women Write More Bad Books than Men?; On the Absence of the Creative Faculty in Women; Domestic Infelicity of Literary Women. Then there are my favorites: Typewriters in the Kitchen; Housewife with an Office; Authoress in an Apron; Playwrights in Petticoats. Needless to say, one does not find critical essays on men writers entitled "Locker Room Lyricist" or "Dramatists in Drawers."

As I completed my work, however, it occurred to me that I had had some preconceptions about what the criticism would be like which were not borne out. I had thought to find some development, or at least clear change, in the criticism over the years. I also expected the criticism to provide illumination and support for my belief that there is a women's tradition in literature, that women, because their lives have been different from men's lives, have written differently.

With regard to historical development, I recently came across the following note which I had made as I began the bibliography: attack→apology→achievement→analysis + anger. This "A theory" meant that I might find a movement from attacks on the idea of women writing, to apologies for women writing, to accounts of their achievements (the latter often being a sort of apology of its own). Then in very contemporary criticism there would be a change of emphasis, with the attack-apology syndrome giving way to real analysis of writing by women and also consideration of restrictions on women writers and discrimination against them. The contemporary criticism, I had also thought, would be more carefully documented, more honest and direct, and less sexist

Since criticism is not written in a vacuum, the A theory could not be totally wrong. With the advent of the current women's movement, there has been an explosion of critical essays on women writers; many of the critics are feminists, angry rather than apologetic, and straightforward in their views. Also, there are some critical attitudes which now seem to be extinct. In the twentieth century one finds fewer writers who go on about "women's sphere" or refer to poetesses as "slatternly" (it is hoped that they do not refer to "poetesses" at all); women are seldom thought of as adding refinement to literature, shedding over the literature of America "a delicate and tender bloom" (No. 168) To some extent one can correlate the critical attitudes and feminist social thought (or lack of it) of the time. For instance, in the 1940's and 1950's, the height of what Kate Millet calls the "counterrevolution," there was less criticism on women writers, and much of what does exist is of the "Typewriters in the Kitchen" type.

Except in very broad and obvious ways, however, the A theory does not hold. If many critics of the 1970's are feminists, there are also many who are not. Recent critics attack women writers as a group just as early critics did, and often with the same tastelessness and cruelty; correspondingly, early critics often indulged in extravagant praise. One finds similar ideas and controversies running through criticism from the 1800's to the present. Doris Grumbach's 1964 article claiming that female novelists have never written anything of value sounds much like Molly Seawell's 1891 essay, which raised such a storm in *Critic*. Tillie Olsen's well-known "Silences: When Writers Don't Write" has many prototypes, some back in the nineteenth century (see, for instance, Nos. 282, 307, and 323). Agnes Repplier was making witty attacks on "phallic criticism" long before Mary Ellmann coined the term; George Parsons Lathrop discussed androgyny in 1890. While some nineteenth-century critics were praising women's refined and delicate touch in literature, others were accusing them of writing obscene novels and lowering the moral tone of literature. That controversy has persisted until the present day; the language may have changed, but not the basic ideas. One would have difficulty, I think, in matching the following statements with their proper publication dates.

> A. 1860's
> B. 1890's
> C. 1930's
> D. 1950's
> E. 1970's

1. Salacious writing by women is one "socially dangerous aspect of the exaggerated 'feminism' that proclaims that 'women are equal to men.' " (No. 174)
2. Works by women are judged not by their merits but according to their "conformity to the codes of sexual behavior laid down for women by society." (No. 317)
3. The average woman of ordinary strength finds it impossible to combine a writing career with housework and childcare. (No. 307)
4. Female novelists are hardened souls who are responsible for today's "empty kitchen" and "empty cradle." (No. 201)
5. Male critics limit the topics upon which women can write and then condemn their work as "tame and commonplace." (No. 323)
6. Women writers express too much anger and create infantile heroines. (No. 193)
7. Writing can serve as an antidote to the fact that woman, "once wound up by the marriage ceremony, is expected to click on with undeviating monotony till Death stops the hands." (No. 395)
8. Female novelists rarely construct realistic male characters, and they dwell on superficial details of dress and appearance. (No. 261)

(Answers: 1-D; 2-C; 3-B; 4-C; 5-A; 6-E; 7-A; 8-E.)

That the last statement is by a feminist critic of the 1970's is not really surprising, for the qualities ascribed to women's writing remain essentially the same throughout the years. According to much of the criticism, women's writing differs from men's in being more emotional and more subjective. It is realistic, carefully detailed, and emphasizes character and relationships above action. Depending on the critic's attitude and resultant choice of language, it is either narrower or deeper in range than literature by men. Many writers, of course, have taken the opposite view and argued that literature by women has nothing in common; one often encounters the statement, "Writing has no sex." Interestingly enough, however, these critics often end up contradicting themselves and referring to "feminine sensibility" or the feminine literary tradition. A contemporary observer summarized the conclusions of the recent Doubleday Women Writers Symposium as "Writing Hath No Sex, BUT. . . ." (No. 233).

Thus on the question of whether women and men write differently, I found confusion rather than the enlightenment I had hoped for. There are many essays, from the 1800's to the present, which are so vacillating they are almost impossible to abstract (see, for instance, Nos. 215 and 402). Others make firm pronouncements which are completely opposite. Take, for example, the case of George Eliot, who seems to be a favorite illustration for every theory. In the course of arguing that female novelists are inferior to male novelists, W. L. Courtney in *The Feminine Note in Fiction* takes care to assure his point by defining any outstanding female novelist as masculine. Thus George Eliot was "essentially a masculine genius, in no respect characteristically feminine. In other words, she was an artist: an ideal which the average female writer finds it difficult to attain." This view of Eliot was no surprise; I remember it being taken out of the closet and aired the few times women writers were mentioned in my undergraduate literary studies. However, in an article called "The Womanliness of Literary Women" (No. 383), whom do we find as the ideal "womanly" novelist, the one who, above all others, brings the "grace of femininity" to her writing? George Eliot, naturally.

Critics will disagree, but one finds bewildering extremes even from critics with the same politics and even in "safe" areas like literary history. Nineteenth-century American women writers were ultra-conservative and conformist / they were angry radicals. Women have been innovators in the field of literature /

they have imitated men. Women have succeeded in writing fiction but failed with other genres / they have written excellent poetry but done poorly elsewhere. One wonders: Have the critics been reading the same books? One also wonders: Whence all the assurance?

After having immersed myself in this contradictory criticism, I began to admit possibilities which would not have occurred to me before. Perhaps women writers could not reasonably be studied as a group. It could be shown that certain female writers influenced others, but there might be no "female tradition." On the other hand, given women's similar history, this view seemed nonsense too. Anything could be true. For instance, I encountered strong agreement among male drama critics and playwrights of different eras that women cannot write great drama because they lack "architectural" ability: They cannot construct plays. Perhaps this theory wasn't as mindless and bigoted as it first appeared; perhaps playing with erector sets rather than dolls in childhood is more than phallic preparation and develops some mysterious faculty of construction needed in writing plays.

I found myself becoming more and more receptive to a comment of Annette Kolodny's: It is time, she says, for feminist critics to stop assuming that women write differently from men (or assuming they don't, one might add) and time to ask how to approach the question; how could we discover if they wrote differently or not? (See No. 360.) Similarly, I am impatient with the never-ending series of essays, some by avowed feminists, entitled "Why Haven't Women Written Great _____?" (Fiction, Poetry, Drama, Tragedy, Epics, what you will.) It seems more reasonable to ask, "Have Women Written Great _____?," or even more reasonably, how could we know if they had or not?

This type of question is new in the criticism on women writers as a group. In one sense, feminist literary criticism is not new; as I have already pointed out, many early critics were consciously feminist in outlook, had the same concerns, and came to many of the same conclusions as critics of the 1970's. What is different in the literary criticism influenced by the current women's movement is the *consciousness* of practicing a certain type of criticism, the attempt to define it, and the attention given to methodology and philosophy. This is a step forward, I think; we may find that many critics have simply been asking the wrong questions.

At any rate, I believe feminist critics can benefit from acquaintance with what has been done in the past (especially before the contemporary women's movement). There are some surprises, as I have noted—the lack of easily discernible patterns, the amount of early work imbued with feminist consciousness, the early (and often weird) studies of women's style. Also, analysis of the existing criticism might yield some rewards when it comes to setting priorities for feminist criticism. Certain areas, such as feminine stereotypes in literature and discrimination against women writers, have already been well-covered and clearly documented. Others, especially those which require some careful attention to method, are quite unsettled and require work before we can move to other critical tasks. It is difficult, for instance, to relate "lost" women writers to the female tradition in literature, or reinterpret well-known writers in light of it, if we do not know what the tradition is or even whether it really exists. Another frequently mentioned task of the new feminist criticism, prescriptive criticism and the attempt to influence the literature of the future, becomes dubious without a clearer concept of the past. Bibliographic work is affected also: More bibliographies on women writers are needed, but their conception can, and I hope will, be based on firmer ground.

AMERICAN WOMEN WRITERS

I. BIOGRAPHY

1. Chase, Mary Ellen. "Five Literary Portraits."
   Massachusetts Review, 3 (Spring 1962),
   511-516.

   Short accounts of her acquaintance with 5
   women writers. Includes Sarah Orne Jewett, Willa
   Cather, and Gertrude Stein.

2. Forrest, Mary. [Julia Deane Freeman.] Women of
   the South Distinguished in Literature. New
   York: Charles B. Richardson, 1865. 511pp.

   Biographical sketches and excerpts from the
   works of 35 Southern writers.

3. Harkins, E. F., and Johnston, C. H. L. Famous
   Authors (Women). Boston: L. C. Page & Co.,
   1901. 343pp. Also printed as part of the
   Little Pilgrimage Series as Little
   Pilgrimages among the Women Who Have Written
   Famous Books. Boston: L. C. Page & Co.,
   1902.

   Chatty biographies of 21 American "story
   writers," representing all sections of the
   country.

4. Hart, John S. The Female Prose Writers of
   America. With Portraits, Biographical
   Notices, and Specimens of Their Writings.
   3rd ed. Philadelphia: E. H. Butler and Co.,
   1857. (1st ed. 1851) 536pp.

   Biographical notices, with characterizations
   of the authors' works and brief excerpts. The
   rationale for the book, given in the preface, is
   that "women, far more than men, write from the
   heart. Their own likes and dislikes, their
   feelings, opinions, tastes, and sympathies are so
   mixed up with those of their subject, that the

1

interest of the reader is often enlisted quite as much for the writer, as for the hero, of a tale."

5. Kirkland, Winifred, and Kirkland, Frances. <u>Girls Who Became Writers</u>. Freeport, N. Y.: Books for Libraries Press, 1971. (1st pub. 1933) 121pp.

    Short, simple biographical essays on 10 writers, 8 of them Americans. Includes popular writers, such as Pearl Buck and Mary Roberts Rinehart, as well as Edna St. Vincent Millay and Willa Cather.

6. Maurice, Arthur B. <u>Makers of Modern American Fiction (Women)</u>. The Mentor, Series No. 185. New York: Mentor Associates, 1919. 25pp.

    Brief description of the lives and works of women writers of the time. There is also some discussion of their precursors, who created a "splendid feminine tradition" in fiction. Includes many excellent portraits.

7. Moore, Virginia. <u>Distinguished Women Writers</u>. New York: E. P. Dutton and Co., 1934. 253pp.

    Short essays on novelists and poets of various countries and time periods. Mainly biographical, but gives some description and assessment of the authors' works.

8. Muir, Jane. <u>Famous Modern American Women Writers</u>. Famous Biographies for Young People. New York: Dodd, Mead & Co., 1959. 171pp.

    Brief, simple biographical sketches of 11 writers, from Emily Dickinson to Eudora Welty.

9. Overton, Grant M. <u>The Women Who Make Our Novels</u>. New York: Moffat, Yard & Co., 1919. (1st pub. 1918) 393pp.

    Essays on popular American writers who were alive in 1918. Each essay gives biographical details, a general critical evaluation, and a list of the writer's published works. Covers 35 novelists, including Edith Wharton, Willa Cather, and Zona Gale.

10. Raymond, Ida. [Mary T. Tardy.] The Living Female
    Writers of the South. Philadelphia: Claxton,
    Remson & Haffelfinger, 1872. 568pp.

    Condensed version of the item below.

11. _____ . Southland Writers: Biographical and
    Critical Sketches of the Living Female Writers
    of the South. With Extracts from Their
    Writings. 2 vols. Philadelphia: Claxton,
    Remson & Haffelfinger, 1870. 973pp.

    Covers 115 writers. The author says she has
    omitted the best-known writers, giving prominence
    to those who were contributors to confederate
    journals.

12. Russell, Hattie Sanford. "A Group of Michigan
    Women Writers." Midland Monthly, 6 (Oct.
    1896), 327-334.

    Biographical sketches of 11 writers, several
    of whom are clubwomen or businesswomen. Includes
    portraits.

13. Spofford, Harriet Prescott. A Little Book of
    Friends. Boston: Little, Brown and Co., 1916.
    184pp.

    Biographies of 10 American women writers.
    Except for the "local colorists," Rose Terry Cooke
    and Sarah Orne Jewett, they are today unknown.

14. Untermeyer, Louis. "The Answering Voice." Ladies'
    Home Journal, 81 (May 1964), 66, 122-126.

    On Sara Teasdale, Elinor Wylie, Amy Lowell,
    Marianne Moore, and Edna St. Vincent Millay.
    Includes personal reminiscences and comments on
    the poets' attitudes toward love. Argues that
    poetry by women does not much differ from poetry
    by men; what female poets have in common is "the
    ability to write poetry."

15. Van Vechten, Carl. "Some 'Literary Ladies' I Have
    Known." Yale University Library Gazette, 26
    (Jan. 1952), 97-116.

    Gossipy account of his acquaintance with
    several writers, including Gertrude Stein, Gertrude
    Atherton, Nella Larson, and Ellen Glasgow.

16. Wharton, Anne Hollingsworth. "A Group of Early
    Poetesses." Colonial Days & Dames.
    Philadelphia: J. B. Lippincott Co., 1898.
    Pp. 99-124.

    Information, mostly biographical, on colonial
    poets, such as Anne Bradstreet, Mercy Warren and
    Elizabeth Graeme Fergusson.

17. Women Authors of Our Day in Their Homes: Personal
    Descriptions & Interviews. Edited by Francis
    Halsey. New York: James Pott and Co., 1903.
    300pp.

    Short interviews with female authors, or
    essays about them, by a variety of writers. Covers
    27 women, including Gertrude Atherton, Elizabeth
    Stuart Phelps, and Mary E. Wilkins. Selections
    emphasize description of the author's house and
    furniture but often consider her motives for
    writing, methods of composition, etc.

See also: 49, 405, 411

4

II. SPECIAL GROUPS

18. Arlt, Gustave O. "California's Literary Women."
    Historical Society of Southern California
    Quarterly, 36 (June 1954), 99-114.

    Account of the lives and works of numerous
    California women writers. Focuses on Ina Donna
    Coolbrith, Gertrude Atherton, and Helen Hunt
    Jackson, whom he considers the major writers.

19. Bernard, Jacqueline. "Mountain Voices:
    Appalachian Poets." Ms., 5 (Aug. 1976), 34.

    Discussion of the lives and works of 4 women
    poets. Their poetry reveals the Appalachian
    woman's "struggle to emerge as her own witness."

20. Cruikshank, Cathy. "Lesbian Literature: Random
    Thoughts." Margins, No. 23 (Aug. 1975),
    40-41.

    Distinguishes between "Lesbian Literature"
    and "Female Homosexual Literature," giving
    examples of both types. The latter shows women
    oppressing women, whereas the former presents women
    interacting with other women on an equal basis.

21. Earle, Alice Morse. "Early Prose." Early Prose
    and Verse. Edited by Alice Morse Earle and
    Emily Ellsworth Ford. New York: Harper &
    Brothers, 1893. Pp. 3-103.

    Introduction to selections from the writings
    of New York women. Discusses the lack of
    educational facilities for women in New York State
    in the seventeenth and eighteenth centuries and the
    variety of male prejudices against women writers.
    Briefly reviews the careers of well-known women
    writers of New York.

22. Edward, Ann, Sister. "Three Views on Blacks: The
        Black Woman in American Literature." <u>CEA
        Critic</u>, 37 (May 1975), 14-16.

        Two views are of the Black heroine as created
by Black and white authors. However, the
discussion is focused on Black women writers, such
as Lorraine Hansberry and Gwendolyn Brooks.

23. Foster, Jeannette H. <u>Sex Variant Women in
        Literature</u>. New York: Vantage Press, 1956.
        412pp.

        Study of literature by or about sex variant
women from early times to the present. "Sex
variant" is never adequately defined by the author
but is usually taken to mean feeling romantic love
or passion for a member of one's own sex. Before
the twentieth century women were prevented from
writing much on the topic, but the author considers
several women writers "whose lives most readily
yield suggestive hints" of variance and correlates
these with "corresponding traces, however carefully
masked, in their writing." In Chapters 9 and 10
she analyzes twentieth-century fiction in English,
and in the last chapter concludes that male critics
have been prejudiced in their literary evaluation
not only of sex variant writing by women but of all
female writings.

24. Foulk, Virginia. "Women Authors of West Virginia."
        <u>West Virginia History</u>, 25 (Apr. 1964),
        206-210.

        Paper read at 1963 meeting of the West
Virginia Historical Society. Describes the major
literary contributions of West Virginia women, from
the early 1800's to the present.

25. Goodwin, Etta Ramsdell. "The Literary Women of
        Washington." <u>Chautauquan</u>, 27 (Sept. 1898),
        579-586.

        Describes the works of several women writers
from Washington, D. C. The best known are
E. D. E. N. Southworth and Frances Hodgson Burnett.

26. Henneman, John Bell. The Nineteenth Century Woman
    in Literature. N. p. [1892]. 25pp.

    Address delivered to the Virginia Literary
    Society of the State Female Normal School of
    Farmville, Va. Women are encouraged to represent
    the life of the South in fiction. Their novelistic
    strength is said to be representation of the
    emotions and insight into details. Southern women
    have excelled especially in description of nature
    and scenery and romantic love.

27. Hilldrup, Robert Le Roy. "Cold War against the
    Yankees in the Antebellum Literature of
    Southern Women." North Carolina Historical
    Review, 31 (July 1954), 370-384.

    Discusses the fiction of Southern women before
    the Civil War. More women than is generally
    realized defended the culture and institutions of
    the South and attacked Northern puritanism and
    commercialism.

28. Hubbell, Jay B. The South in American Literature,
    1607-1900. Durham, N. C.: Duke University
    Press, 1954. 987pp.

    Section 38, pp. 602-610, is on women writers.
    In the 1840's and 1850's authorship was one of the
    few occupations open to women, and a considerable
    number of Southern women began writing. They were
    generally better educated than their Northern
    counterparts, lived in urban areas, had strong
    economic motives for writing, and often used
    pseudonyms because of prejudice against women
    writers. "The place which Southern women writers
    made for themselves they made in spite of the
    disapproval of literary critics and often of timid
    and skeptical publishers." There is a great deal
    of information on individual Southern women writers
    in the rest of the book.

29. Margins, No. 23 (Aug. 1975).

    Special issue entitled "Focus: Lesbian
    Feminist Writing & Publishing." Contains essays,
    book reviews, poems, and letters on the topic.

30. Mersand, Joseph. "Jewish Poets in America in the Nineteenth Century." Traditions in American Literature: A Study of Jewish Characters and Authors. Port Washington, N. Y.: Kennikat Press, 1968. (1st pub. 1939) Pp. 118-127.

   On Penina Moise, Emma Lazarus, and Adah Isaacs Menken. Discusses their poetry and their pride in their "racial and religious heritage." When Jewish men of letters remained silent about the treatment of Jews in other parts of the world, these poets spoke out.

31. Mimi and Tanya. "Lesbian Writers Come Together." Off Our Backs, 5 (Nov. 1975), 18.

   Account of the Second Annual Lesbian Writers' Conference, held in Chicago in September, 1975. Discusses many issues in lesbian writing and literary criticism, for instance, the need to develop variety and go beyond coming-out stories and the need to "determine a standard of lesbian-feminist writing." Women must create a criticism based on insight, rather than the competition and "nihilistic slashing" of male criticism.

32. Molette, Barbara. "They Speak: Who Listens? Black Women Playwrights." Black World, 25 (Apr. 1976), 28-34.

   Few listen, because Black women playwrights are at the mercy of the media brokers, most of whom are white males; these men wish to prevent certain truths about Black female experience from being exposed. Also, plays by Black women have been misinterpreted by biased critics. In order to change the situation, Black women need to assume positions of power in the theater and mass communications media.

33. "The Negro Woman in American Literature." Keeping the Faith: Writings by Contemporary Black Women. Edited by Pat Crutchfield Exum. Greenwich, Conn.: Fawcett Publications, 1974. Pp. 19-40. Originally published in Freedomways, 6 (Winter 1966), 8-25.

   Panel discussion held during conference on "The Negro Writer's Vision of America" at the New School for Social Research in 1965. Sarah E. Wright, Abbey Lincoln, Alice Childress, and Paule

8

Marshall discuss the stereotyped portraits of Black
women in the works of male writers and the need for
Black women writers to create complex human
characters. Paule Marshall emphasizes the
difficult position of the Black woman writer in a
society which takes neither women nor Blacks
seriously.

34. Parks, Adrienne. "The Lesbian Feminist as Writer
    as Lesbian Feminist." Margins, No. 23
    (Aug. 1975), 67-69.

    Argues that in the past women writers
subscribed to male-determined forms for fiction and
poetry. However, contemporary Lesbian feminist
writers are "concerned with women's perceptions
derived from women's experiences" and are creating
new forms and content.

35. Reid, Mary J. "Four Women Writers of the West."
    Overland Monthly, 24 (Aug. 1894), 138-144.

    On poets Ina D. Coolbrith (Cal.) and Edith M.
Thomas (Ohio) and fiction writers Alice French
(Iowa) and Mary N. Murfree (Tenn.). Notes that
female writers of the West keep within conventional
lines and are "opposed to the most rugged types of
Western virility."

36. Robbins, Mary La Fayette. Alabama Women in
    Literature. Selma, Ala.: Selma Printing Co.,
    1895. 209pp.

    Description of the activities of women's
literary clubs, selections from writings by
Alabama women, and commentary by Robbins. Sees a
"striking contrast" between past and present
literature by Alabama women. Higher education and
"the exigencies of a more complex life" have
developed women's writing abilities.

37. Rule, Jane. Lesbian Images. New York: Pocket
    Books, 1976. (1st pub. 1975) 257pp.

    Intelligent and sensitive exploration of the
images of lesbians found in fiction, biography and
autobiography by lesbian writers. In her study of
12 individual writers the author finds very
different images, emphasizing "the individuality
and variety of lesbian experience." In her survey

9

of lesbian novels of the last 40 years she detects
a move from apology to protest and more positive
portrayal of lesbianism.

38. Sanborn, Kate. "New England Women Humorists." New
       England Magazine, N. S. 35 (Oct. 1906), 155-
       159.

       Brief descriptions of the humorous writings
    of several New England women. Notes that humor in
    the works of female authors is given less
    recognition than it deserves.

39. Shange, Ntozake. "Black Women Writing/ Where
       Truth Becomes Hope/ Cuz It's Real." Margins,
       No. 17 (Feb. 1975), 50-54, 59-60.

       Discussion of novels by Ann Petry, Nella
    Larson, and Zora Neale Hurston. Black women can
    write freely only when they have "grown thru the
    wounds & humiliations" of being Black, poor and
    female.

40. Skeeter, Sharyn J. "Black Women Writers: Levels
       of Identity." Essence, 4 (May 1973), 58-59,
       76, 89.

       Historical survey of fiction by Black women,
    with attention to images of Black womanhood. Ends
    with an account of contemporary Black women
    writers. Since the 1960's they have taken more
    initiative and are becoming "a considerable force
    in Afro-American literature."

41. Smith, Thelma M. "Feminism in Philadelphia,
       1790-1850." Pennsylvania Magazine of History
       and Biography, 68 (July 1944), 243-268.

       Survey of the achievements of Philadelphia
    women writers. Discusses their education and
    interests and the influence of feminist social
    thought on their careers and writings.

42. Stanley, Julia P. "Uninhabited Angels: Metaphors
       for Love." Margins, No. 23 (Aug. 1975), 7-10.

       Discussion of fiction by and about Lesbians.
    In novels prior to 1970 the characters are
    "uninhabited angels," satisfied with images of

themselves created by others. After 1970 there is
an "important shift in the conceptual structures
of Lesbian novels," with the omniscient narrator
abandoned and the characters speaking in their
own voices, without guilt and self-hatred.

43. Stimpson, Mary Stovell. "Radcliffe Women in
Literature and Drama." New England Magazine,
N. S. 39 (Oct. 1908), 223-237.

Survey of the literary accomplishments of
Radcliffe graduates. Includes a large number of
portraits.

44. Toth, Susan Allen. "Sarah Orne Jewett and Friends:
A Community of Interest." Studies in Short
Fiction, 9 (Summer 1972), 233-241.

Speculates about the personal relationships
between Jewett and 3 other New England "local
colorists," Rose Terry Cooke, Mary E. Wilkins
Freeman, and Alice Brown. Jewett knew all of them,
and they wrote fiction with similar settings and
characters for the same audience. Concludes that
"they must have formed a genuine community of
interest that was valuable to all of them." Also,
the 4 writers "provide in the history of American
literature a seldom-heard voice proclaiming the
occasional joys of being a single woman."

45. Tutwiler, Julia R. "The Southern Woman in New
York." Bookman, 18 (Feb. 1904), 624-634;
19 (Mar. 1904), 51-58.

Considers the typical experience of the
Southern woman who comes to New York in hopes of
succeeding in the literary world. Then discusses
the works and New York experiences of specific
Southern writers, such as Ruth McEnery Stuart and
Mary Virginia Terhune.

46. Walker, Alice. "In Search of Our Mothers'Gardens."
Ms., 2 (May 1974), 64-70, 105.

Discusses the creativity of Black women of the
past, "the agony of the lives of women who might
have been Poets, Novelists, Essayists, and Short
Story Writers (over a period of centuries), who
died with their real gifts stifled within them."
Believes that these women have "handed on the

creative spark to their daughters and
granddaughters."

47. Washington, Mary Helen. "Black Women Image
       Makers." Black World, 23 (Aug. 1974), 10-18.

       Essay on fictional heroines of Black women
writers. Exhorts Black readers to go beyond
rejecting stereotyped images of Black women in the
white media and give their attention to the
realistic portraits of Black women in the writings
of Gwendolyn Brooks, Alice Walker, Maya Angelou,
Paule Marshall, and Toni Cade Bambara.

48. _____. "Introduction." Black-eyed Susans:
       Classic Stories by and about Black Women.
       Edited by Mary Helen Washington. Garden City,
       N. Y.: Anchor Books, 1975. Pp. ix-xxxii.

       Discussion of black women writers' "special
and unique vision of the black woman" and their
treatment of several themes: adolescence, physical
beauty, alienation between black and white women,
mother-daughter conflict, and antagonism between
black women and black men.

49. "Women Fiction Writers of Maine." Maine Library
       Bulletin, 14 (July 1928), 8-24.

       Essay tracing the history of women's writing
in Maine, followed by biographical sketches of the
principal Maine women writers and lists of their
work.

50. Yee, Carole Zonis. "Why Aren't We Writing about
       Ourselves?" Images of Women in Fiction:
       Feminist Perspectives. Edited by Susan
       Koppelman Cornillon. Bowling Green, Ohio:
       Bowling Green University Popular Press, 1972.
       Pp. 131-134. Also in Off Our Backs (Feb.-Mar.
       1972).

       Calls for Jewish women to write literature
embodying their experiences as women and as Jews.
Jewish women are teaching in universities and
writing feminist essays, but if readers look for
characters in fiction who represent the modern

Jewish woman, they find only the spoiled, selfish
castrators imagined by Jewish males.

See also: 2, 10, 11, 12, 240, 287

III. SPECIAL TOPICS

51. Bonner, Geraldine. "Women and the Unpleasant
         Novel." Critic, 48 (Feb. 1906), 172-175.

         Claims that contemporary female novelists
    have a "curious predilection for subjects which are
    morbid, unpleasant, or of a sultry equatorial
    warmth." The reason is that women are drawn
    instinctively to regions of sentiment and passion,
    but domestic sentiment has been overworked and
    the domestic environment is "an unfortunately
    circumscribed area." Thus women have gone to the
    other extreme and chosen shocking subjects.

52. Bruère, Martha Bensley, and Beard, Mary Ritter,
         eds. Laughing Their Way: Women's Humor in
         America. New York: Macmillan Co., 1934.
         295pp.

         Anthology of humor, with comments by the
    editors and a brief introduction to the life and
    work of each author included. Many of the humorous
    passages are from fiction, and there are sections
    on the humor of the nineteenth-century domestic
    novelists and the "local colorists" of the South.

53. Canby, H. S. "The Feminine Touch in Literature."
         American Estimates. New York: Harcourt, Brace
         and Co., 1929. Pp. 205-213.

         Complains that, although many of the best
    novelists in America are women, "the feminine
    touch upon literature is not favorable to man in
    fiction." Male writers have lavished their genius
    upon women, creating memorable heroines, but female
    writers are not fair to men. "They persist in
    studying him in only an aspect, only in his love
    relationships." It is acceptable for men novelists
    to present women exclusively in this light because
    women "reach almost invariably their fullest
    expressiveness" when in love, but men lead broader
    lives.

14

54. Duvall, Ellen. "Women's Heroes." Atlantic, 90
    (Dec. 1902), 831-834.

    Criticizes female novelists for creating
    unconvincing heroes. Women's heroes are never
    allowed wit and humor, and they are presented as
    idealized lovers rather than complex, seemingly
    actual men.

55. Earls, Michael. "Three Poets in a Golden Clime."
    Catholic World, 142 (Jan. 1936), 551-561.

    Considers religious elements in the poetry of
    Katharine Tynan, Louise Imogen Guiney, and Dora
    Sigerson. Also discusses the friendship of the 3
    poets and includes excerpts from their letters.

56. "The Ethics of Popularity." Saturday Review of
    Literature, May 9, 1936, p. 8.

    Summarizes the disagreement between Gerould
    and Banning (see #58 and #322)and remarks on the
    unfortunate split between popular and "serious"
    literature.

57. Gelderman, Carol W. "The Male Nature of Tragedy."
    Prairie Schooner, 49 (Fall 1975), 220-226.

    Asks why no woman has ever written great
    tragedy and concludes that "all the conditions of
    her life are hostile to the state of mind which is
    needed to create great tragedy." Tragedy is a
    public art, whereas women are forced to be private;
    women are "enfeebled" by their conditioning and
    cannot perceive the possibility of "intrepid,
    audacious, self-reliant personages."

58. Gerould, Katharine Fullerton. "Feminine Fiction."
    Saturday Review of Literature, Apr. 11, 1936,
    pp. 3-4, 15. Discussion, May 9, 1936, p. 8.

    Discussion of "escape literature" written by
    women for female readers. This fiction is "very
    materialistic," being devoted to descriptions of
    clothing, food, and household items. Since its
    main purpose is to allow every reader to identify
    with the heroine, the female characters tend to be
    "faceless mannequins." See #56 and #322.

    Discussion - Applies thesis to detective fiction.

59.   Gilder, Jeannette L. "Some Women Writers."
          Outlook, Oct. 1, 1904, pp. 281-289.

          Account of the works of some new writers of
      the time. Stresses female humorists and says that
      more women are writing humorous fiction than ever
      before.

60.   Gustafson, Richard. "'Time Is a Waiting Woman':
          New Poetic Icons." Midwest Quarterly, 16
          (Spring 1975), 318-327.

          On new images of time in current poetry by
      women. In Sylvia Plath and Diane Wakoski time is
      represented by a militaristic father figure, but
      Adrienne Rich and Robin Morgan "seem to be creating
      the ghost of a future figure," a female image of
      time.

61.   Harris, Janice H. "Our Mute Inglorious Mothers."
          Midwest Quarterly, 16 (Spring 1975), 244-254.

          Notes that our literature contains few images
      of mothers and children viewed from the mother's
      perspective. This is because "compared to men,
      women have written little; but women with children
      have written scarcely at all." The option to
      write has not been open to them, and mothers have
      been hampered by their own limited expectations.

62.   Heilbrun, Carolyn. Toward a Recognition of
          Androgyny. New York: Alfred A. Knopf, 1973.
          189pp.

          Defines androgyny as "a condition under which
      the characteristics of the sexes, and the human
      impulses expressed by men and women, are not
      rigidly assigned." Traces androgynous themes and
      characters through literature, with frequent
      discussion of women writers. Contemporary women
      writers are writing feminist, rather than
      androgynous, novels, but Heilbrun believes "great
      androgynous works will soon be written."

63.   Holliday, Robert Cortes. "Why Men Can't Read
          Novels by Women." Walking-Stick Papers. New
          York: George H. Doran Co., 1918. Pp. 159-170.

          Because they "present a singularly insular
      travesty of man, an unconscious caricature."

Women's portrayal of male characters is colored by
an aversion to masculine qualities and a
sentimental worship of feminine ones. The theme of
most of our recent fiction by women is "peevish
criticism of husbands." As these sentiments are
attributed to a "friend" of the writer, a gruff
Colonel, there is an outside chance that male
critics are being satirized.

64. Johnsen, William A. "Modern Women Novelists:
        Nightwood and the Novel of Sensibility."
        Bucknell Review, 21 (Spring 1973), 29-42.

        Argues that the modern feminine "novel of
sensibility," as represented by Djuna Barnes'
Nightwood, allows women to criticize "man's
totalitarian obsession to impose order everywhere."
However, it is a trap which makes women "more
perfect victims of categorization by fulfilling
stereotypical feminine roles."

65. Lupton, Mary Jane, and Toth, Emily. "Out, Damned
        Spot!" Ms., 2 (Jan. 1974), 97-99.

        Deals with references to menstruation in
literature. Until recently the few references made
have generally been negative: menstruation has been
seen as a sign of female inferiority or
irrationality. Now that many women have stopped
accepting men's evaluation of their bodily
processes, feminist writers have begun to treat
menstruation in literature.

66. Lyons, Harriet. "Female Eroticists: Stirrings of
        Sexuality." Village Voice, Apr. 27, 1972,
        pp. 1, 24, 26, 42.

        Account of recent erotic literature and art
"by women for women." Erotica has heretofore been
a male specialty, but now feminists are offering
"subjective, graphic and unromanticized" portraits
of sexual experience.

67. Manley, Seon, and Lewis, Gogo. "Introduction."
        Grande Dames of Detection: Two Centuries
        of Sleuthing Stories by the Gentle Sex.
        Edited by Seon Manley and Gogo Lewis. New

York: Lothrop, Lee & Shepard Co., 1973.
Pp. 11-13.

Discussion of women's contributions to
detective fiction.

68.   Manley, Seon, and Lewis, Gogo. "Introduction."
      Ladies of Fantasy: Two Centuries of Sinister
      Stories by the Gentle Sex. Edited by Seon
      Manley and Gogo Lewis. New York: Lothrop, Lee
      & Shepard Co., 1975. Pp. 1-2.

      Considers why women writers have long been
      interested in the world of fantasy. Speculates
      that even the most successful writers were
      "chained by realities a man did not know"
      (housework, childcare, etc.) and thus "found a
      creative liberation in worlds of fantasy." Women
      also "have always had a remarkable sensitivity for
      areas of intuition."

69.   _____. "Introduction." Ladies of the Gothics:
      Tales of Romance and Terror by the Gentle Sex.
      Edited by Seon Manley and Gogo Lewis. New
      York: Lothrop, Lee & Shepard Co., 1975.
      Pp. 11-12.

      Discusses women's pioneering efforts in both
      strains of Gothic writing, romance and the
      supernatural.

70.   _____. "Introduction." Mistresses of Mystery:
      Two Centuries of Suspense Stories by the
      Gentle Sex. Edited by Seon Manley and Gogo
      Lewis. New York: Lothrop, Lee & Shepard Co.,
      1973. P. [11].

      Brief mention of women's accomplishments in
      the development of the mystery story.

71.   _____. "Introduction." Sisters of Sorcery:
      Two Centuries of Witchcraft Stories by the
      Gentle Sex. Edited by Seon Manley and Gogo
      Lewis. New York: Lothrop, Lee & Shepard Co.,
      1976. Pp. 9-10.

      Notes that women writers have frequently
      explored the world of witchcraft and have handled
      traditional themes in untraditional ways.

72. Manley, Seon, and Lewis, Gogo. "Introduction."
    Women of the Weird: Eerie Stories by the
    Gentle Sex. Edited by Seon Manley and Gogo
    Lewis. New York: Lothrop, Lee & Shepard Co.,
    1976. Pp. 9-10.

    Claims that "women have always had a strange
    gift for the weird, a talent for the unknown, the
    unseen." Women developed the ghost story as a
    genre and brought it to its zenith.

73. Maurice, Arthur Bartlett. "Feminine Humorists."
    Good Housekeeping, 50 (Jan. 1910), 34-39.

    Short descriptions of the works of American
    women humorists of the time. Contends that the
    newest generation of women writers is less
    sentimental than the old and has more sense of
    humor.

74. Mizejewski, Linda. "Sappho to Sexton: Woman
    Uncontained." College English, 35 (Dec.
    1973), 340-345.

    Discussion of escape imagery in the poetry of
    Sappho, Emily Dickinson, Sylvia Plath, and Anne
    Sexton. They portray the "woman uncontained," the
    woman "broken off, flying into night, swept into
    air."

75. Moers, Ellen. "Female Gothic: Monsters, Goblins,
    Freaks." New York Review of Books, Apr. 4,
    1974, pp. 35-39.

    Continues her examination of the female
    Gothic tradition, begun in Mar. 21, 1974 issue.
    The earlier article, "Female Gothic: The Monster's
    Mother," deals with the beginning of the Gothic
    tradition in England. This essay treats later
    writers, including some Americans. The persistence
    of the Gothic mode into our own time is accounted
    for by "the self-disgust, the self-hatred, and the
    impetus to self-destruction that have been, alas,
    increasingly prominent themes in the writing of
    women in the twentieth century."

76. Moers, Ellen. "Money, the Job, and Little Women."
    Commentary, 55 (Jan. 1973), 57-65.
    Discussion, 55 (May 1973), 26.

    Contends that money and its making were
    characteristic female, rather than male, subjects
    in nineteenth-century fiction in English.
    Discusses Jane Austen, Charlotte Bronte, Harriet
    Beecher Stowe, and Louisa May Alcott. In *Uncle*
    Tom's Cabin Stowe related slavery to the cash nexus
    of American society; in *Little Women* work plays a
    large part.

77. Morgan, Ellen. "Humanbecoming: Form & Focus in the
    Neo-Feminist Novel." *Images of Women in*
    Fiction: Feminist Perspectives. Edited by
    Susan Koppelman Cornillon. Bowling Green,
    Ohio: Bowling Green University Popular Press,
    1972. Pp. 183-205.

    Discusses 3 novelistic forms which are being
    affected by the new feminism: the *bildungsroman*,
    the historical novel, and the propaganda novel.
    Emphasizes the *bildungsroman*, or apprenticeship
    novel. Traditionally it has been a male form, but
    feminists are adapting it in order to "express the
    emergence of women from cultural conditioning into
    struggle with institutional forces, their progress
    toward the goal of full personhood." Discusses
    Alix Kates Shulman's *Memoirs of an Ex-Prom Queen*
    as an example.

78. Mussell, Kay J. "Beautiful and Damned: The Sexual
    Woman in Gothic Fiction." *Journal of Popular*
    Culture, 9 (Summer 1975), 84-89.

    Discussion of female characters in modern
    gothic fiction by women. Two types of women are
    portrayed: the heroine, who conforms to
    traditional feminine role expectations, and the
    "other" woman, who does not conform and is thereby
    punished. The rivalry and distrust between the
    two types reinforces "women's identification with
    and dependence upon men."

79. Pratt, Annis. "Women and Nature in Modern
    Fiction." *Contemporary Literature*, 13 (Aug.
    1972), 476-490.

    Compares modern fictional works by female and
    male writers. Concludes that the heroines of Sarah

Orne Jewett, Ellen Glasgow, Willa Cather, Doris
Lessing, etc. take a different approach to nature
than the heroes in novels by men.

80. Rather, Lois. "Were Women Funny? Some 19th
    Century Humorists." American Book Collector,
    21 (Feb. 1971), 5-10.

    Survey of female humor, with discussion of
such writers as Ann Stephens, Marietta Holley,
and Frances Whitcher. Notes that female
humorists are seldom represented in anthologies
and humor magazines and vacillates between
concluding that women are lacking in humor and
accusing male editors of prejudice.

81. "Reflections on Science Fiction: An Interview with
    Joanna Russ." Quest, 2 (Summer 1975), 40-49.

    Russ discusses feminism in science fiction
and answers yes to the question, "Can women science
fiction writers play a political role in the field
of science fiction and within the women's
movement?" She believes the most important task
for the female science fiction writer, and female
artist in general, is to shift the "center of
gravity from Him to Me."

82. Rollins, Alice Wellington. "Woman's Sense of
    Humor." Critic, Mar. 29, 1884, pp. 145-146.

    Contends that there are no deliberately
humorous female characters in men's novels
because men writers cannot create humor as well as
women can. Gives examples of humor in literature
by women.

83. Russ, Joanna. "The Image of Women in Science
    Fiction." Images of Women in Fiction:
    Feminist Perspectives. Edited by Susan
    Koppelman Cornillon. Bowling Green, Ohio:
    Bowling Green University Popular Press, 1972.
    Pp. 79-94. Also in Vertex, 1 (Feb. 1974),
    53-57.

    Notes that most science fiction is written by
men for men, and the women characters are
stereotypes. Science fiction by women contains
"more active and lively female characters than do
stories by men, and more often than men writers,

women writers try to invent worlds in which men
and women will be equals." However, women science
fiction writers are not free from stereotyping and
prejudice against women.

84. Russ, Joanna. "Outta Space: Women Write Science
        Fiction." Ms., 4 (Jan. 1976), 109-111.

        Contends that, after Mary Shelley's
Frankenstein, the first science fiction novel,
science fiction became "a man's game, like rockets,
war, space travel, and all other future
possibilities." But beginning in the late 1960's
the field has seen an influx of women writers, many
of them feminists.

85. _____. "Somebody's Trying to Kill Me and I
        Think It's My Husband: The Modern Gothic."
        Journal of Popular Culture, 6 (Spring 1973)
        666-691.

        Analyzes the typical plot patterns and
character types of the modern gothic written by
women for women. The gothic is "a direct
expression of the traditional feminine situation"
and provides the perfect escape reading for the
"middle-class believer in the feminine mystique."

86. Sanborn, Kate, ed. The Wit of Women. 4th ed. New
        York: Funk and Wagnalls Co., 1895. (1st ed.
        1885) 215pp.

        Collection of puns, epigrams, and humorous
sketches by women, with introduction and running
commentary. Emphasizes American writers.
Sanborn resents statements by men that humor is a
rare quality in women and attempts to show that
although "the wit of women has been almost utterly
ignored and unrecognized," women are not deficient
in wit and humor.

87. Sargent, Pamela. "Introduction." More Women of
        Wonder: Science Fiction Novelettes by Women
        about Women. Edited by Pamela Sargent. New
        York: Vintage Books, 1976. Pp. xi-liii.

        Discusses recent science fiction which
explores the role of women, difficulties women
have had in publishing science fiction, and
possibilities for improving the genre. Also

considers the representation of childbirth and homosexuality in science fiction.

88. Sargent, Pamela. "Introduction: Women in Science Fiction." Women of Wonder: Science Fiction Stories by Women about Women. Edited by Pamela Sargent. New York: Vintage Books, 1975. (1st pub. 1974) Pp. xiii-lxiv.

Substantial introduction to women writers and characters of science fiction. Includes historical survey of female science fiction writers from Mary Shelley to the present. Also speculates on the role science fiction can play in providing women with "possible scenarios for their own future development."

89. Sauder, Rae Norden. "They Kill and Tell." Independent Woman, 21 (Oct. 1942), 303, 317-318.

Account of women mystery writers, their motivation, work methods, and accomplishments. Quotes an editor as saying women have the edge over men in the detective novel field. "The hard-boiled school is on the wane, and they [women] have a knack for full-bodied detective stories that stand up as novels."

90. Spacks, Patricia Meyer. "Free Women." Hudson Review, 24 (Winter 1971-72), 559-573.

One theme in the works of modern "emancipated" women who have written about themselves is the "persistent impossibility of feminine freedom." Revised and considerably expanded version of the essay appears as Chapter VIII in Spacks' book, The Female Imagination.

91. _____. "Taking Care: Some Women Novelists." Novel, 6 (Fall 1972), 36-51.

Discusses the theme of the cost of a "happy marriage" with its focus on "taking care," as presented in several novels by American and English women writers. "Taking care" is often used as a means of power and control. Expanded version of the essay appears as Chapter III in Spacks' book, The Female Imagination.

92. Stein, Karen F. "Reflections in a Jagged Mirror:
    Some Metaphors of Madness." <u>Aphra</u>, 6 (Spring
    1975), 2-11.

    Discussion of the "mad" heroine and the mirror
    as symbol in several works, including Charlotte
    Perkins Gilman's <u>The Yellow Wallpaper</u> and Sylvia
    Plath's <u>The Bell Jar</u>. The function of the "mad"
    woman character, who uses periods of inner turmoil
    to plumb her personal depths and then returns to
    the world of normality, is to question and
    challenge societal norms and sex roles.

93. Stout, Rex. "These Grapes Need Sugar." <u>Vogue's</u>
    <u>First Reader</u>. New York: Julian Messner, 1942.
    Pp. 421-425.

    Attempt at humor, at the expense of women
    writers. A law should be passed "prohibiting
    females from writing detective stories." Women
    have an "inveterate and universal habit of
    personalizing," and thus their murders are genteel
    and their detectives sissies. The indictment
    includes Dorothy Sayers and Agatha Christie, as
    well as several American women mystery writers.

94. Suckow, Ruth. "Literary Soubrettes." <u>Bookman</u>, 63
    (July 1926), 517-521.

    Contrasts the fictional heroines of male and
    female authors. In books by men the heroines often
    carry a "smothering burden of idealization." Women
    create more individual female characters, but
    sometimes they show an unfortunate "teachery
    Sunday School attitude" toward their heroines. The
    worst error the woman writer can make is "using her
    heroine for the purposes of self-pity and self-
    justification."

95. "Symposium: Women and Tragedy." <u>Prairie Schooner</u>,
    49 (Fall 1975), 227-236.

    Four responses to Carol Gelderman's question,
    "Why has no woman ever written great tragedy?"
    (see #57). It is suggested that women have been
    denied the necessary "realization of the self" and
    that they fail to attain aesthetic distance. One
    reason given is "because, living it, she never had
    a chance." It is also proposed that women have,
    in fact, written great tragedy, but not tragic

drama because they were not writing when drama
was the prevailing mode.

96. Teasdale, Sara. "Foreword." The Answering Voice:
Love Lyrics by Women. Edited by Sara
Teasdale. New York: Macmillan Co., 1928.
Pp. ix-xiii.

Introduction to revised and enlarged edition
of her anthology of women's love poetry (see
below). Detects a "change of mood" in women's
love poems written since 1917. The treatment of
love is less conventional, and there is a wider
range of feeling, with less dependence on the
beloved and less despair.

97. _____. "Prefatory Note." The Answering Voice:
One Hundred Love Lyrics by Women. Edited by
Sara Teasdale. Boston and New York: Houghton,
Mifflin and Co., 1917. Pp. ix-x.

Contends that women have done their best
creative work in poetry, and in most cases "the
finest utterance of women poets has been on love."

98. Toth, Emily. "Women and Their Friends." Women: A
Journal of Liberation, 3, No. 2 (1972), 44.

Notes that the feminist critical approach
changes the questions we ask about literature. One
important question is how female characters relate
with each other. In some works traditionally
considered feminist, such as Lysistrata, they
compete and judge each other by male standards, but
in Sylvia Plath's The Bell Jar and Kate Chopin's
The Awakening women have strong and close
relationships.

99. Tucker, Martin. "Introduction." Confrontation,
No. 7 (Fall 1973), 79-81.

Introduction to "The Woman Writes" issue.
Asks whether women can understand men and write
about them as well as men can. Claims that the
magazine requested essays on the question of women
writers' creation of male characters, but most
women declined. Thus, women writers must be
"puzzled and unclear about the revolution."

100. Viorst, Judith. "What Men Do to Women--What Women
     Do to Themselves." Redbook, 142 (Feb. 1974),
     46-51.

     Considers the theme of "woman as victim" in
recent fiction by women. In many novels the
heroine is portrayed as used and abused because
of her need for men.

101. Watson, Barbara Bellow. "On Power and the Literary
     Text." Signs, 1 (Fall 1975), 111-118.
     Discussion, 1 (Summer 1976), 1005.

     Finds in the analysis of some fiction by women
an escape from the dilemma of "two polarized
abstractions" about power. That is, certain
feminists believe women should seize every power
base they can, others think women should eschew
power. In novels by Virginia Woolf, Doris Lessing,
and Kate Chopin, however, women are found
exercising power based on ability and energy and
not on dominance. This suggests the possibility
that women can exercise power without "forgetting
the lessons of the outsider." Watson comments
throughout on the "descriptive and analytic
functions" of feminist criticism; feminist
criticism can provide us with a method of reading
with broader consciousness.

102. "Women Novelists and the Bow-wow." Current
     Literature, 30 (Feb. 1901), 215.

     Contends that female writers have excelled
at every type of fiction except romance. The
reason is that women are interested in character,
while romance stresses action and demands the
reduction of characters to types. "Possibly
romance . . . is a product of the masculine
temperament, as the finest and minutest
characterization is of the feminine."

103. "Women's Men." Saturday Review of Literature,
     Nov. 8, 1974, p. 257.

     Argues that the male characters of female
writers differ from the male characters of male
writers. Women can and sometimes do create "men's
men," but generally their heroes are more
emotional. A woman's "interest will spring more

sharply toward the instinctive than toward the
rational type."

See also: 14, 38, 48, 117, 127, 179, 240, 309, 313, 329,
           338, 380, 404

IV. LITERARY HISTORY

104. Auchincloss, Louis. Pioneers & Caretakers: A Study
        of 9 American Women Novelists. Minneapolis:
        University of Minnesota Press, 1965. 202pp.

        Essays on Sarah Orne Jewett, Edith Wharton,
        Ellen Glasgow, Willa Cather, Elizabeth Madox
        Roberts, Katherine Anne Porter, Jean Stafford,
        Carson McCullers, and Mary McCarthy. To
        Auchincloss women "have always been the true
        conservatives, the caretakers of the culture."
        From this premise it is but a short step to
        considering women writers as part of a single
        tradition--conservatism and caretaking. American
        women writers are also more "affirmative" than the
        men and more "nostalgic."

105. Beard, Mary Ritter. "American Women and the
        Printing Press." Annals of the American
        Academy of Political and Social Science, 143
        (May 1929), 195-206.

        Attempt at "evaluation of the writing by
        American women as a whole." The positive
        accomplishments she describes are almost entirely
        in the field of fiction; at other types of writing
        women have done less well because they are not
        learned enough.

106. Beer, Thomas. "The Titaness." The Mauve Decade.
        New York: Alfred A. Knopf, 1926. Pp. 17-61.

        An attack on American women of the late
        nineteenth century, satirizing Louisa May Alcott
        and other female writers of the time.

107. Benson, Mary Sumner. Women in Eighteenth-Century
        America: A Study of Opinion and Social Usage.

New York: Columbia University Press, 1935.
Pp. 118-119, 170-171, 188-193, 209-222.

Facts on conditions for women writers in the eighteenth century. Discusses some early novels and contributions to women's periodicals.

108. Bernikow, Louise. "Introduction." The World Split Open: Four Centuries of Women Poets in England and America, 1552-1950. Edited by Louise Bernikow. New York: Vintage Books, 1974. Pp. 3-47.

Extensive discussion of the inadequacies of male critics and biographers and the alienation of female poets from male culture. Includes two separate historical surveys, one of poetry by English women and one of poetry by American women.

109. Bode, Carl. "The Scribbling Women: The Domestic Novel Rules the 'Fifties." The Anatomy of American Popular Culture, 1840-1861. Berkeley, Cal.: University of California Press Press, 1959. Pp. 169-187.

Compares the domestic novel of the mid-1800's with the "soap opera" of today and concludes that it "satisfied certain basic needs of the unconscious" as well for its time as the serials do today. Analyzes several of the most popular novels by women in attempt to show that they all contain 5 of the main Jungian archetypes: the anima, the animus, the earth mother, the old wise man, and the self as child.

110. Bogan, Louise. "The Heart and the Lyre." A Poet's Alphabet: Reflections on the Literary Art and Vocation. Edited by Robert Phelps and Ruth Limmer. New York: McGraw-Hill Book Co., 1970. Pp. 424-429.

Essay, written in 1947, on the "rise and development of female poetic talent" in America. Surveys the past in terms of the question of whether female poets imitated men. Concludes that far from imitating men poets, women experimented boldly with form and language. Ironically, it is the contemporary women poets who seem to be following male trends. Because of "contemporary pressures or mistaken self-consciousness," they are denying the intensity of emotion which is the key to female poetic talent.

111. Brown, Herbert Ross. The Sentimental Novel in America, 1789-1860. Durham, N. C.: Duke University Press, 1940. 407pp.

Much of the book concerns women novelists, but the chapters "Sex and Sensibility" and "Home, Sweet Home" are particularly relevant. Contains detailed descriptions of novels by women; emphasizes their "intense concern with marriage."

112. Cowie, Alexander. "The Domestic Sentimentalists and Other Popular Writers (1850-1870)." The Rise of the American Novel. New York: American Book Co., 1948. Pp. 412-446.

Summaries of the lives and works of 10 popular women writers. Includes amusing "recipe for a domestic novel," which illuminates its typical plot pattern. Individual women writers of the nineteenth century are discussed in other parts of the book.

113. _____. "The Vogue of the Domestic Novel, 1850-1870." South Atlantic Quarterly, 41 (Oct. 1942), 416-424.

Early version of the above. Treats the domestic novel generally, without going into detail about individual novelists. Emphasizes the conservatism of the women writers, claiming that they were against reform movements. They argued against women's rights and, although they believed slavery was wrong, portrayed abolitionists unfavorably.

114. Dexter, Elisabeth Anthony. "With Tongue, Pen, and Printer's Ink." Colonial Women of Affairs: A Study of Women in Business and the Professions in America Before 1776. Boston and New York: Houghton, Mifflin and Co., 1924. Pp. 126-179.

Discussion of the lives and works of women writers of the colonial period.

115. Ernest, Joseph M., Jr. "Whittier and the
        'Feminine Fifties.'" American Literature,
        28 (Mar. 1956-Jan. 1957), 184-196.

        Claims John Greenleaf Whittier is due
  substantial credit for the success of American
  women writers after 1850. Discusses Whittier's
  encouragement of struggling writers and his
  influence on the careers of such women as Lucy
  Larcom, Elizabeth Stuart Phelps, E. D. E. N.
  Southworth, and Sarah Orne Jewett.

116. "The Female Poets of America." North American
        Review, 68 (Apr. 1849), 413-436.

        Review of recent anthologies of poetry.
  Stresses women's contributions to poetry and
  attempts to trace the "gradual improvement in
  taste and composition" from the first women poets
  in America to contemporary poets such as Sarah
  Josepha Hale. Female poets have "a finer
  susceptibility and more ready sympathies" than
  male poets.

117. Forrey, Carolyn. "The New Woman Revisited."
        Women's Studies, 2, No. 1 (1974), 37-56.

        Discusses the portrayal of the "new woman"
  by 8 American women novelists in the 1880's and
  90's. The "new woman" is shown rejecting
  marriage for a career or personal independence and
  having to face an unresolvable dilemma. "While
  she is the embodiment of a desire for freedom, the
  social roles available to her deny that freedom,
  demanding rigid adherence to convention."

118. Frederick, John T. "Hawthorne's 'Scribbling
        Women.'" New England Quarterly, 48
        (June 1975), 231-240.

        Summarizes the 5 best-selling novels by
  American women published from 1850-1855, the period
  just preceding Hawthorne's famous letter decrying
  the "damned mob of scribbling women." Also
  discusses women's contributions to and editorship
  of magazines during the period and surmises that
  Hawthorne resented female journalists as much as
  female novelists.

31

119. Hardwick, Elizabeth. Seduction and Betrayal: Women
and Literature. New York: Random House, 1974.
208pp.

Collection of essays, some expanded from the
original version in New York Review of Books. One
essay is on Ibsen's female characters, the others
on women writers. It is still unclear why the
book is subtitled "Women and Literature" because
the author believes that "every artist is either a
man or a woman and the struggle is pretty much the
same for both." Sex is irrelevant: Virginia Woolf
put too much emphasis on her femininity; Zelda
Fitzgerald's problem was that she resembled her
husband in personality; it is inconceivable how
Sylvia Plath could have gone mad.

120. Harned, Mary. "Early Women Poets of America."
Poet Lore, 5 (June 1893), 332-341.
Discussion, 5 (Oct. 1893), 531-532.

General discussion of poetry written by
American women in the seventeenth and eighteenth
centuries. Emphasizes Anne Bradstreet, Phyllis
Wheatley, Mercy Warren, Susannah Rowson, and
Margaretta V. Faugères.

121. Hart, James D. "Home Influence." The Popular
Book: A History of America's Literary Taste.
New York: Oxford University Press, 1950.
Pp. 85-105.

Account of the nineteenth-century domestic
novelists. Brief discussion of the works of Maria
Cummins, Fanny Fern, E. D. E. N. Southworth, and
other women writers of the time.

122. Heller, Shirley H. 20th Century American Women
Authors: A Feminist Approach: A Critical
Commentary. Monarch Notes. New York:
Monarch Press, 1975. 92pp.

Summarizes the lives and works of 15 fiction
writers, from Edith Wharton to Erica Jong.
Outlines a "feminist approach" to a major work
by each author. Includes study questions and
background on images of women in literature before
the twentieth century.

123. Higginson, Thomas Wentworth. "Woman in
     Literature." Woman: Her Position, Influence,
     and Achievement throughout the Civilized
     World. Edited by William C. King.
     Springfield, Mass.: The King-Richardson Co.,
     1901. Pp. 493-505.

     Essay on the literary position of women in the
classical period and the modern period in Europe
and America. Provides a short survey of American
women writers considered the most important at the
time. Concludes that "all modern society has,
until a very recent period, been incredulous and
repressive in dealing with intellectual women,
and it is a satisfaction to think that it is in the
English-speaking nations as a whole that more
sympathy has been bestowed on them."

124. Hopkins, Percie Trowbridge. "On Female Poets."
     Poet Lore, 30 (Dec. 1919), 588-595.

     Discusses several poets praised by Griswold
in 1848 (see #238) and quotes from their works.
Except for the earliest poets, such as Anne
Bradstreet and Phyllis Wheatley, he finds the
poetry tedious.

125. Jacobsen, Josephine. "From Anne to Marianne:
     Some Women in American Poetry." Two
     Lectures. Washington: Library of Congress,
     1973. Pp. 13-29.

     Lecture delivered at the Library of Congress
on May 1, 1972. Traces the atmosphere in which
female poets worked from the time of Anne
Bradstreet to the present. Poets in the period
from Bradstreet to Emily Dickinson could not fully
realize their talents; the chief elements in
their attitudes were "those one might expect from a
body of literate, highly privileged slaves." In
the period from Dickinson to Marianne Moore "the
entire paralyzing structure of the attitude toward
women writers had begun to show cracks, and then
gaps." However, poets like Elinor Wylie and Edna
St. Vincent Millay still lacked the freedom of the
contemporary female poet.

126. Jessup, Josephine Lurie. The Faith of Our
      Feminists. New York: Biblo and Tannen, 1965.
      128pp.

      Study of Edith Wharton, Ellen Glasgow, and
Willa Cather. Feminism in their works is taken to
mean the existence of women characters of great
strength and endurance. This one aspect of the
novels is heavily emphasized.

127. Kaplan, Cora. "Salt and Bitter and Good." Salt
      and Bitter and Good: Three Centuries of
      English and American Women Poets. Edited by
      Cora Kaplan. New York: Paddington Press Ltd.,
      1975. Pp. 13-25.

      Substantial introduction to anthology of
women's poetry. The title is taken from the
following lines of Elizabeth Barrett Browning,
which are seen as a manifesto for women poets:
"Weep and write./ A curse from the depths of
womanhood/ Is very salt, and bitter, and good."
Considers "how women poets fought to express a view
of the world and the self that was singular to
their sex but as comprehensive as any male
perspective." Includes discussion of critics'
treatment of female poets and an analysis of
flower imagery in poetry by women.

128. Lawrence, Margaret. The School of Femininity: A
      Book for and about Women as They Are
      Interpreted through Feminine Writers of
      Yesterday and Today. Port Washington, N. Y.:
      Kennikat Press, 1966. (1st pub. 1936) 382pp.

      Treats nineteenth-century English and
twentieth-century English and American writers.
The modern women novelists are put in rather odd
categories, such as "Little Girl Pals,"
"Go-getters," "Priestesses," and "Artistes." The
style of the book is also odd, seemingly an
imitation of Gertrude Stein. Lawrence considers
the writing of women "distinctively feminine" in
both "psychological current" and technique. The
feminist movement of the early twentieth century
was an important and beneficial influence on the
work of women.

129. Loshe, Lillie Deming. The Early American Novel.
New York: Columbia University Press, 1907.
131pp.

Study of the American novel between 1789 and
1830. Important source of information on women
writers of the time; includes discussion of the
novel of seduction and such writers as Susanna
Rowson and Hannah Webster Foster.

130. Manley, Seon, and Belcher, Susan. O, Those
Extraordinary Women: or the Joys of Literary
Lib. Philadelphia: Chilton Book Co., 1972.
330pp.

Odd literary history, as can be seen from the
title of the book and the titles of some of the
chapters: "The Moor Was Mightier than the Men: The
Brooding Brontes"; "The Pens That Rocked the Cradle
and the World: Louisa May Alcott and Harriet
Beecher Stowe." Covers English and American
women writers from the time of Mary Wollstonecraft
to the 1930's. The authors' attempts at humor are
unfortunate, and their tone is condescending;
however, there is a wealth of quotations from early
women writers and nineteenth-century illustrations.

131. Manthorne, Jane. "The Lachrymose Ladies." Horn
Book, 43 (June 1967), 375-384; (Aug. 1967),
501-513; (Oct. 1967), 622-630.

Patronizing account of nineteenth-century
American women who wrote bestselling novels.
Focuses on attitudes and fictional heroines of
Susan Warner, Maria Cummins, and Martha Finley.

132. Moers, Ellen. Literary Women: The Great Writers.
New York: Doubleday & Co., 1976. 336pp.

Collection of essays held loosely together by
a common subject: the "major women writers" of
America, England, and France. The approach is
neither consistently historical nor theoretical;
the author calls her study "a celebration of the
great women who have spoken for us all." Several
chapters, such as "Female Gothic," appeared
previously as articles but are here considerably
revised and expanded. There are chapters on
various types of "heroinism" and an interesting
essay on metaphors and "female landscapes" which
recur in women's fiction. Appended to the text is

a selected checklist of literary women including names, dates, nationalities, and chronology of works.

133. Moers, Ellen. "Women's Lit: Profession and Tradition." *Columbia Forum*, 1 (Fall 1972), 27-34.

Claims that women writers have their own tradition. Their sex has "canceled out . . . otherwise major differences of language, religion, class, and period, and brought into close and productive relationship women writers who never could . . . meet face to face." They have read each other's works closely and influenced each other. Examples are taken from English, American, and French writers, primarily of the nineteenth century.

134. Monroe, N. Elizabeth. *The Novel and Society: A Critical Study of the Modern Novel*. Port Washington, N. Y.: Kennikat Press, Inc., 1965. (1st pub. 1941) 282pp.

On 6 women novelists, Sigrid Unset, Selma Lagerlof, Edith Wharton, Ellen Glasgow, Virginia Woolf, and Willa Cather. Thesis is that the novel as an art form has decayed, but these writers have managed to "retain human values in the midst of decadence." The author feels called upon to apologize for treating women writers. "This is not to set up a brief for woman in the novel. The novel is concerned with human beings, not with man or woman, so that the sex of the novelist is not a determining factor in his art or in the criticism of it." This statement is, however, contradicted several times in the space of the book.

135. Papashvily, Helen Waite. *All the Happy Endings: A Study of the Domestic Novel in America, the Women Who Wrote It, the Women Who Read It, in the Nineteenth Century*. New York: Harper & Brothers, 1956. 231pp.

Study of popular novels written by ordinary women of the century. Contains much useful information. Contends that the domestic novels were "handbooks of feminine revolt," communicating female grievances beneath the surface.

136. Pattee, Fred Lewis. The Feminine Fifties. Port
     Washington, N. Y.: Kennikat Press, 1966.
     (1st pub. 1940) 339pp.

     Social and literary history of the 1850's in
     America. Considers the decade "feminine" because
     it was "fervid, fevered, furious, fatuous, fertile,
     feeling, florid, furbelowed, fighting, and funny."
     In Chapters V and IX, which deal exclusively with
     women writers, "scribbling women" are alternately
     patronized and attacked.

137. Petter, Henri. The Early American Novel.
     Columbus, Ohio: Ohio State University Press,
     1971. 500pp.

     Covers American novels from 1775 to 1820.
     Updates Loshe's study (#129) and also includes much
     material on women writers. There is a whole
     chapter devoted to Susanna Rowson and another on
     Tabitha Tenney's Female Quixotism.

138. Saul, George Brandon. Quintet: Essays on Five
     American Women Poets. Studies in American
     Literature, Vol. XVII. The Hague,
     Netherlands: Mouton & Co., 1967. 50pp.

     On Sara Teasdale, Elinor Wylie, Hazel Hall,
     Abbie Huston Evans, and Winifred Welles. Contends
     that these poets, who wrote in the early part of
     the twentieth century, have been neglected by
     recent critics and deserve more serious attention.

139. Schulman, Grace. "Women the Inventors." Nation,
     Dec. 11, 1952, pp. 594-596.

     Argues that many of the "inventors" of
     English and American literature have been women.
     "Inventors," as defined by Pound, are "discoverers
     of a particular process or of more than one mode
     and process." Women have been founders of many
     literary genres and precursors of literary trends.
     Brief examples are given, though more space is
     needed for adequate support of the thesis.

140. Smith, Harrison. "Feminism and the Household
    Novel." Saturday Review, Mar. 30, 1957,
    p. 22.

    Brief summary of the work of female novelists
of the 1850's and 60's. Does not mention feminism
and inaccurately portrays the "household
novelists" as having led "sheltered domestic
lives."

141. Smith, Henry Nash. "The Scribbling Women and the
    Cosmic Success Story." Critical Inquiry, 1
    (Sept. 1974), 47-70.

    Examines popular American fiction, mainly
novels by women, between the early 1850's and the
early 1870's. This fiction expresses the "ethos
of conformity"; unquestioned submission to
authority is shown to lead to success. Does not
relate this thematic pattern to the situation of
women.

142. Smith, Leslie. "Through Rose-Colored Glasses:
    Some American Victorian Sentimental Novels."
    New Dimensions in Popular Culture. Edited by
    Russell B. Nye. Bowling Green, Ohio: Bowling
    Green University Popular Press, 1972.
    Pp. 90-106.

    Discusses the "rags to riches" pattern in
some popular American novels of the middle
nineteenth century. Emphasizes novels by
E. D. E. N. Southworth and Mary Jane Holmes.

143. Sprague, Rosemary. Imaginary Gardens: A Study of
    Five American Poets. Philadelphia: Chilton
    Book Co., 1969. 237pp.

    On Emily Dickinson, Amy Lowell, Sara Teasdale,
Edna St. Vincent Millay, and Marianne Moore. There
is an essay on each, combining biography and
criticism and followed by a selection of poems.

144. Stanford, Ann. "Introduction." The Women Poets
    in English: An Anthology. Edited by Ann
    Stanford. New York: McGraw-Hill Book Co.,
    1972. Pp. xxix-xlix.

    Introduction to anthology of English and
American poetry representing over 100 female poets

from Anglo-Saxon times to the present. Reviews
the history of poetry by women, discussing
important individuals and trends. Emphasizes
poetry written before the twentieth century.

145. Taylor, William R., and Lasch, Christopher. "Two
         'Kindred Spirits': Sorority and Family in New
         England, 1839-1846." New England Quarterly,
         36 (Mar. 1963), 23-41.

         Attempts to explain "the longing of women for
literary careers" in the 1830's and 1840's by
examining the friendship of 2 ordinary women,
Louella J. B. Case and Sarah Edgarton. Concludes
that women were pursuing "an ideal of pure
friendship between women, based on a shared
sensitivity," and they found it in common devotion
to literature.

146. Thompson, Adele E. "Woman's Place in Early
         American Fiction." Era, 12 (Nov. 1903),
         472-474.

         Discussion of American women writers from
Anne Bradstreet to Harriet Beecher Stowe. The
earliest writers, who concentrated on poetry and
religious prose, were "a little thin and somewhat
lacking in originality." However, when women
began writing fiction they were more successful
and built the foundation for later novelists.

147. Urann, C. A. "Early Women Writers in America."
         Chautauquan, 30 (Jan. 1900), 377-380.

         Favorable review of women's literary
accomplishments in the nineteenth century ("early"
means early 1800's). As the century progressed,
women learned "to look deeper into their subjects,
to handle them with greater skill and to be less
easily swayed by their emotions."

148. Voloshin, Beverly. "A Historical Note on Women's
         Fiction: A Reply to Annette Kolodny."
         Critical Inquiry, 2 (Summer 1976), 817-820.

         Attempt to "correct a historical
misconception" in Kolodny's article on feminist
criticism (#360). Kolodny mistakenly implies that
once Nathaniel Hawthorne became acquainted with the
novels of his female contemporaries he reversed his

earlier negative judgment. In fact, he later
praised only Ruth Hall, which differs greatly from
other women's novels of the time; few readers today
will be able to work up much enthusiasm for these
novels.

149.   Waller, Jennifer R. "'My Hand a Needle Better
       Fits': Anne Bradstreet and Women Poets in the
       Renaissance." Dalhousie Review, 54 (Autumn
       1974), 436-450.

       Argues that Anne Bradstreet and women poets
       in English of the sixteenth and seventeenth
       centuries "share characteristics which make up a
       recognizable if loosely linked tradition." They
       are uneasy and apologetic about invading a
       traditionally male field, and their work shows the
       effects of a limited education. However, like the
       domestic novelists, they often find inspiration in
       their restricted domestic environment and in so
       doing gain originality and depth.

150.   Wasserstrom, William. Heiress of All the Ages: Sex
       and Sentiment in the Genteel Tradition.
       Minneapolis: University of Minnesota Press,
       1959. 157pp.

       Social and literary history of the genteel
       tradition, covering the period between the 1830's
       and World War I. Emphasizes women readers and
       fictional heroines over women writers but includes
       valuable background material for study of the
       writers.

151.   Wellington, Amy. Women Have Told: Studies in the
       Feminist Tradition. Boston: Little, Brown,
       and Co., 1930. 204pp.

       Essays on American and English feminist
       writers, including the Brontes, Margaret Fuller,
       and Charlotte Perkins Gilman. One interesting
       essay, "Militancy and Ellen Glasgow," attempts to
       relate the late nineteenth-century split in the
       American woman's movement to the literature of the
       time.

152.   "Women." Senior Scholastic, Mar. 4, 1946, p. 15.

       Claims that the greatest poets have been male
       but women have excelled in writing short lyrics.

In illustration, discusses the poetry of Sara
Teasdale and Elinor Wylie.

153. Wood, Ann D. "The Literature of Impoverishment:
          The Women Local Colorists in America
          1865-1914." Women's Studies, 1, No. 1 (1972),
          3-40.

          Argues that, in rejecting the feminine
      literary tradition established by the
      sentimentalists, the "local colorists" were
      regressing rather than progressing. The
      sentimentalist sensibility was aggressive and
      feminist; the pre-civil war novelists dealt, albeit
      in a disguised way, with the power struggle between
      the sexes. However, for the local colorists "the
      act of writing offered an exercise in nostalgia
      or a release for despair rather than a vehicle for
      a covert power play." They were not revolutionary
      and retreated from life. Argument relies on
      premise that covert power struggles are
      revolutionary.

154. _____. "The 'Scribbling Women' and Fanny Fern:
          Why Women Wrote." American Quarterly, 23
          (Spring 1971), 3-24.

          Discusses the ambivalence of mid-nineteenth-
      century American women writers. Most women felt
      guilty about "taking over a man's field and
      enjoying the conquest" and thus, with the support
      of male reviewers, tried to justify their work as
      morally elevating. They downplayed their economic
      motives and finally thought of themselves as
      writing because they could not help it. Fanny Fern
      was an exception and in her writings exposed the
      ambition, economic motives, anger, and bitterness
      against men her peers were striving to conceal.
      Wood calls Fanny Fern "hysterical" and satirizes
      the "atmosphere of male cruelty" in female novels
      of the time.

155. Ziff, Larzer. "An Abyss of Inequality: Sarah Orne
          Jewett, Mary Wilkins Freeman, Kate Chopin."
          The American 1890's. New York: Viking Press,
          1966. Pp. 275-305.

          Deals with Constance Cary Harrison, Mary
      Austin, Gertrude Atherton, and Ellen Glasgow, as
      well as the writers named. The "abyss of
      inequality" is not what one might expect, but the

abyss noted by Henry James between the American woman preoccupied with culture and the American man immersed in business. Ziff contends that "to be a serious female author in the nineties was to be a writer of stories about women and their demands." To him this means that "the woman novelist was trapped by her affiliations to her sex."

See also: 6, 16, 18, 23, 24, 27, 28, 30, 37, 39, 40, 41,
            42, 44, 46, 52, 76, 80, 88, 188, 240, 252,
            267, 282, 291, 315, 326, 369, 408

V. CONTEMPORARY ASSESSMENTS

156. "Are American Women Writing Better Novels than the
     Men?" Literary Digest, July 12, 1924, p. 59.

         Yes, according to an opinion expressed in a
     recent book review. The women "know life better"
     than the men and have fewer illusions; they also
     write more carefully since their motivation is not
     primarily economic.

157. Bergonzi, Bernard. "Mixed Company." New York
     Review of Books, June 3, 1965, pp. 19-20.

         Claims that nineteenth-century women writers
     were interested in the community as well as the
     individual, but contemporary women writers keep
     their focus too narrow. Also, "in a fervor of
     emancipated zeal," they have accepted the premise
     that sex is more important than money.

158. Breuer, Elizabeth. "The Flapper's Wild Oats."
     Bookman, 57 (Mar. 1923), 1-6. Discussion,
     57 (June 1923), 480-481.

         Finds few talented women among the younger
     generation of writers and attributes this lack to
     women's passivity. Women should become more
     aggressive and be willing to give up love, family,
     and social well-being for art.

     Discussion - Jean Starr Untermeyer protests that
     women have not been allowed "peace and privacy"
     for writing.

159. Celarier, Michelle. "Women's Poetry: Personal
     Politics." Northwest Passage, Apr. 22, 1974,
     pp. 12-14.

         Review of recent anthologies of poetry by
     women. Says that female poets are moving away
     from the "defeatism" of Sylvia Plath. They are

"screaming angrily" and "writing everything which it means to be female (and remaining alive)."

160.　Collins, Joseph. "Gentlemen, the Ladies! Four Women Writers Who Have Contributed Substantially to Our Literature." New York Times Book Review, Dec. 23, 1923, pp. 10, 23.

On Edith Wharton, Agnes Repplier, Ellen Glasgow, and Amy Lowell. American women writers are accomplishing as much as the men writers, and Wharton and Repplier are "our most precious literary ornamentation."

161.　Crain, Jane Larkin. "Feminist Fiction." Commentary, 58 (Dec. 1974), 58-62. Discussion, 59 (May 1975), 22-24.

Discusses recent popular feminist novels, such as Sue Kaufman's Diary of a Mad Housewife, Alix Kate Shulman's Memoirs of an Ex-Prom Queen, and Erica Jong's Fear of Flying. Sees them as following many of the "standard conventions of 'ladies' fiction'"--for example, emphasis on the details of housekeeping and "one-sided absorption in the woman's point of view, especially when that point of view is one of helplessness." The characters are unwilling to take any initiative; the novels "reek of the hatred of women."

Discussion - Three letters, all noting that Crain holds different standards for women writers than for men writers.

162.　Dale, Alan. "Women Playwrights: Their Contribution Has Enriched the Stage." Delineator, 90 (Feb. 1917), 7, 42-43.

Asks why there are few contemporary women playwrights, when in the past female dramatists were very successful. Concludes that contemporary theatre is pessimistic, whereas women are optimistic. Also, the female dramatist tends to drop out; "usually she marries and forgets her histrionic triumphs." Discusses some recent women playwrights and concludes that they are most successful when they avoid "the grooves trodden by men" and write domestic plays about marriage and divorce.

163. Davis, H. L. "Enter the Woman." Poetry, 30
     (Sept. 1927), 338-346.

     Book review which consists primarily of
general remarks on the contemporary "transference
of poetry from the estate of men to that of women."
Men are preoccupied with business and have
abandoned the poetic calling. Women, as "impotent
observers of society," are now our poets, and they
are changing the nature and texture of poetry.
"Scrupulous and honorable exactness" is taking the
the place of "creative passion."

164. "Do Women Write More Bad Books than Men?" Current
     Literature, 44 (Jan.-June, 1908), 45-46.

     "Bad" means "indecent." Notes a growing
number of complaints that fiction is becoming
immoral and female authors are largely to blame.

165. Duffy, Martha. "An Irate Accent." Time, Mar. 20,
     1972, pp. 98-99.

     Argues that "writing talent has no gender,"
but for years male critics have viewed women as
writing delicate miniatures about domestic customs
and love. Today's serious women writers are
clearly writing more about hate. They are
producing "fiction with an irate accent," with
the major theme being men's mistreatment of women.

166. "Editor's Study." Harper's, 121 (Oct. 1910),
     799-802; (Nov. 1910), 961-964.

     Last two parts in a series which began in the
Jan. 1910 issue. Having dealt previously with
women's part in the development of the novel, the
editor now surveys contemporary fiction. American
women are seen as "pioneers in realism" and authors
of the "vital fiction" of the time.

167. "Evenings with Some Female Poets." American Whig
     Review, 14 (Sept. 1851), 217-226; (Nov. 1851),
     418-427.

     Evaluation of contemporary poetry by American
women, written in the form of a dialogue. One man
claims women should "look after the domestic,
instead of the poetic fire"; the other disagrees.
Certain poems by women are praised, but in general

female poets are seen as sentimental, imitative, and lacking substance.

168. "Female Literature of the Present Age." Ladies' Garland, Apr. 15, 1837, p. 12.

Brief notice about women's growing contribution to American literature. In earlier ages women wrote little because of their limited education and the constraints of custom; however, "the gentle influence of feminine genius now sheds over the whole literature of our country a delicate and tender bloom."

169. Field, Louise Maunsell. "Heroines Back at the Hearth." North American Review, 236 (Aug. 1933), 176-183.

Same theme as her earlier article below. At the turn of the century American heroines were often portrayed as ambitious and career conscious, but in recent fiction career women are ignored. Both male and female writers have retreated from modern life.

170. _____. "What's Wrong with the Women?" North American Review, 232 (Sept. 1931), 274-280.

Complains that contemporary women writers are out of step with the times. They retreat from portrayal of modern women and instead create heroines who are home and family centered, do not earn their own living, and remain remote from the world of ideas.

171. Fishel, Elizabeth. "End of the Waltz: The Rise of the Feminist Novel." Human Behavior, 5 (June 1976), 64-69.

Discussion of feminist novels which appeared since her 1973 article recounting obstacles in the way of the woman writer (see #285). Although obstacles persist, the feminist novel is on the rise. Feminist writers are using new techniques and creating new heroines, who are no longer "victims, suicides, helpless yearners." Thus far, however, the heroines undergo individual awakenings and do not "embody the sisterhood and collectivity dreamed of by the Women's Movement."

172. "Five Important Playwrights Talk about Theatre
      without Compromise & Sexism." Mademoiselle,
      75 (Aug. 1972), 288-289, 386-387.

      Interview with 5 women, who discuss their
   formation of the Women's Theatre Council and their
   efforts to combat discrimination against female
   playwrights, directors, and producers. The
   playwrights believe they reflect a particular
   sensibility in their plays and speak of the
   affinity they feel for each other's work.

173. Ford, Mary K. "Some Recent Women Short-Story
      Writers." Bookman, 27 (Apr. 1908), 152-161.

      Discusses short stories by American women
   writers of the time; Willa Cather is the only one
   known today. American women are said to excel in
   short story writing, eclipsing American men and
   English and French women.

174. [Gardiner, Harold C.] "When They're Bad They're
      Horrid." America, Sept. 22, 1956, p. 585.
      Also in In All Conscience: Reflections on
      Books and Culture. Garden City, N. Y.:
      Hanover House, 1959. Pp. 215-217.

      Censures the "literary lasciviousness" of
   contemporary female authors. Salacious writing by
   women is "one socially dangerous aspect of the
   exaggerated 'feminism' that proclaims that 'women
   are equal to men.'"

175. Gordi, Tooni. "Foreword." Contemporary American
      Women Poets. Edited by Tooni Gordi. New
      York: Henry Harrison, 1936. Pp. [4-5].

      Claims that female poets of the past "wrote
   on trivialities." Their scope was too narrow and
   their work marred by "sentimentality and
   subjectivism." Contemporary women poets have a
   broader outlook and a "real cognizance of the
   contemporary scene." Women writers still need to
   search for "greater themes."

176. Hendin, Josephine. "Problems of Intimacy: Will We
        Go from Vulnerability to Violence?" *Ms.*, 5
        (Nov. 1976), 66-68, 91.

        Discussion of recent "protest fiction" by
women. Far from being a "weepy complaint," this
fiction reflects "the diversity of our attempts to
cope with anger and reduce our vulnerability." The
weapons of the contemporary woman novelist are a
devastating wit and irony.

177. Hergesheimer, Joseph. "The Feminine Nuisance in
        American Literature." *Yale Review*, 10 (July
        1921), 716-725. Discussion, *Bookman*, 54
        (Sept. 1921), 31-34.

        Emphasizes women readers of fiction over women
writers but sees both as having set the standards
for and determined the tone of the contemporary
American novel. This novel is cheap, sentimental
and not masculine enough. Unfortunately, "women
like the poor are always with us," but "literature
in the United States is being strangled with a
petticoat."

Discussion - Frances Noyes Hart contends that
female readers encourage good literature and female
writers are free of the sentimentality attributed
to them by Hergesheimer.

178. Herrick, Robert. "A Feline World." *Bookman*, 69
        (Mar. 1929), 1-6.

        Criticizes recent female novelists for writing
for women rather than men and for being preoccupied
with emotional subtleties; they are obsessed by sex
and too indirect and "feline" in method. Misses
the action and talk of "standard fiction"--the talk
in the old smoking rooms where "women never
intruded" and one could get a "good male drink."

179. Jameson, Storm. "Love's Labors Exposed." *Atlas*,
        12 (July 1966), 53-54.

        Asks why so many contemporary women novelists
are "writing at dreadful length about their or
their characters' erotic needs and activities."
It cannot be the latest stage in the liberation of
women because the "anxiously free" heroines are
"caught in their sexuality like flies in treacle."
Jameson thinks this type of fiction is boring.

180. Jones, Llewellyn. "The Younger Women Poets."
     English Journal, 13 (May 1924), 301-310.

     Asserts that the younger women poets of the
     day are as good as the younger men poets and
     provide an "even more interesting revelation of
     personality." Edna St. Vincent Millay, Genevieve
     Taggard, Louise Bogan, and Elinor Wylie present a
     picture of the young American woman as alienated
     from her society; civilization has not yet caught
     up with her.

181. Killian, Linda. "Feminist Theatre." Feminist Art
     Journal, 3 (Spring 1974), 23-24.

     Defines feminist theater as "theater written
     by women which tries to explore the female psyche,
     women's place in society, and women's potential."
     Focus of the article is on the work of the West-
     beth Playwrights Feminist Collective and the
     Women's Interart Center.

182. Laurel. "Toward a Woman Vision." Amazon
     Quarterly, 2 (Dec. 1973), 18-42.

     Exhorts women to reject male culture and
     create their own. Until very recently women who
     were privileged enough to become writers gained
     only "the right to explore the impossibilities of
     the male value system and a speedy ticket to
     despair." Susan Sontag, Doris Lessing, and Joan
     Didion are examples. Now women-identified writers,
     such as Robin Morgan and Adrienne Rich, are
     writing out of a "womanvision" about "the
     awakening of women and the salvaging of the earth."

183. Lowell, Sandra. "New Feminist Theater." Ms., 1
     (Aug. 1972), 17-23.

     Account of various feminist theater groups.
     Describes new plays by women, especially those by
     playwright Myrna Lamb.

184. McCracken, Elizabeth. "The American Woman of
     Letters." Outlook, Apr. 9, 1904, pp. 883-889.

     Argues that "the distinctive quality of the
     work of the American woman of letters is the
     vividness and force of its characterization."
     Because they stress character over plot, women have

49

tended to use the short story form. Also, the
fiction of American women has peculiarly American
qualities; like the work of Sarah Orne Jewett, it
is "national in spirit."

185. Mackay, Barbara. "Women on the Rocks." Saturday
         Review World, Apr. 6, 1974, pp. 48-49.

         Review of several recent plays by women.
      Complains that much of this drama presents
      traditional female stereotypes and portrays women
      as victims and losers. Calls for female
      playwrights to create "a revised image of woman,
      proud of her sex and determined to solve her
      problems by some method other than suicide."

186. Mansfield, Margery. "Foreword." American Women
         Poets 1937. Edited by Margery Mansfield.
         New York: Henry Harrison, 1937. Pp. [3-4].

         Introduction to extensive poetry collection.
      Observes that women, because of family obligations,
      are seldom able to devote full time to poetry.
      However, their output is large and most of it is
      good. Contemporary American women poets "produce
      more good poems than could be produced, in the
      same period of time, by any little group of famous
      living poets of either sex, or of both sexes."

187. Matthews, Brander. "On Certain Recent Novels by
         American Women." Cosmopolitan, 10 (Apr.
         1891), 764-768.

         Discusses some female novelists of the day,
      especially Mrs. Burton Harrison and Mrs. Whitney.
      Notes that the field of fiction now belongs as
      much to women as to men.

188. Moers, Ellen. "The Angry Young Women." Harper's,
         227 (Dec. 1963), 88-95.

         Complains that contemporary women writers are
      "complacent and pedantic" beside the Victorian
      women writers. Modern women write too much short,
      timid fiction about the home scene, while the
      Victorians were "angry young women" who wrote
      epic novels, bold and radical. Victorian women,
      ignoring any "special feminine sensibility,"
      invented the industrial novel and emphasized the
      fact that women are an oppressed minority.

189. Monroe, Harriet. "Comment: Men or Women?"
      Poetry, 16 (June 1920), 146-148.

      Asks whether poetry is a masculine or
feminine art. Although she has been "accused" of
publishing more women than men in Poetry, the
majority of the contributors are male. Men are
more interested in writing poetry, and they submit
less "hopelessly bad" verse than women do. "The
modern woman has yet to prove her equality as a
creative artist."

190. _____. "A Few Women Poets." Poetry, 26 (Sept.
      1925), 326-339. Also in Poets & Their Art
      as "Voices of Women." New York: Macmillan Co.
      Co., 1932. Pp. 141-154.

      Survey of the achievements of female poets of
the time. Divides them into 2 classes, the
subjective and the objective, the first expressing
their own emotions and the second expressing the
emotions of others. Believes that in the 1920's
there was "little imitation of men, almost none of
that envious reaching-out for virility which
female artists have often been guilty of"; instead,
women's poetry was noted for "the frank sincerity
of its revelation of the feminine point of view."

191. Muller, Herbert J. "Virginia Woolf and Feminine
      Fiction." Saturday Review of Literature,
      Feb. 6, 1937, pp. 3-4, 14-16.

      Brief discussion of Woolf's fiction "as a
springboard from which to plunge into disagreeable
generalization." The generalization is that
"feminine fiction" is too insubstantial and lacks
vitality. Contemporary writers like Willa Cather,
Ellen Glasgow, and Edith Wharton "brew genteel
tempests in exquisite teapots," while "the mere
man still yearns for a little red beef and port
wine."

192. Nathan, George Jean. "Playwrights in Petticoats."
      American Mercury, 52 (June 1941), 750-755.
      Also in The Entertainment of a Nation, or
      Three-sheets in the Wind as "The Status of the
      Female Playwrights." New York: Alfred A.
      Knopf, 1942. Pp. 34-41.

      Reviews several plays by contemporary
American women and concludes that the best female

playwrights "fall immeasurably short" of the
best masculine playwrights. Female dramatists
possess a "generic feminine inability . . . to
hold the emotions within bounds" and cannot treat
their leading characters and themes objectively.

193.   Peer, Elizabeth. "Sex and the Woman Writer."
          Newsweek, May 5, 1975, pp. 70-72, 73-77.

          Negative view of contemporary American women
writers, who are seen as expressing too much anger
and creating "infantile" heroines. Emphasis is on
the writers' "breaking the taboos" in portraying
the sex lives of their heroines. A caption refers
to Erica Jong as "A Lusty Lady with Talent, Too,"
and we learn from the article that Jong is a
"small, pleasantly rounded" blonde.

194.   Perinciolo, Lillian. "Feminist Theater: They're
          Playing in Peoria." Ms., 4 (Oct. 1975),
          101-104.

          Listing of feminist theatre groups, with
information about contemporary women playwrights.

195.   Phelps, William Lyon. "Famous Women in
          Contemporary Literature." World Review,
          May 7, 1928, pp. 216-217.

          Evaluation of the fiction of Edith Wharton,
Willa Cather, Zona Gale, and other American
novelists of the time. Contends that America has
the best female novelists in the world. There has
never been a great woman composer or poet, but
women can write novels because "fiction, although
a creative art, is also to a certain extent
imitative, repertorial, interpretative."

196.   _____. "A Literary Mystery." Delineator, 120
          (Jan. 1932), pp. 12, 59.

          The mystery is that contemporary British women
writers have not equalled the accomplishments of
their forerunners, whereas in America the situation
is reversed. Novelists like Edith Wharton, Willa
Cather, and Zona Gale are producing better fiction
than the female writers of other countries or
female writers of the American past. Phelps sees
no explanation for the mystery.

197. Pierce, Lucy France. "Women Who Write Plays."
     World Today, 15 (June 1908), 725-731.

     Account of female dramatists of the time, with
     descriptions of their plays. Contends that women
     have become "a recognized power in the drama," in
     spite of initial prejudice against them; of 100
     recognized contemporary playwrights, 30 are women.
     Women have been successful because they are more
     emotional and intuitive than men, being quicker to
     "sense dramatic effectiveness." Article also
     discusses the exclusion of women from the American
     Dramatists' Club and their subsequent formation of
     the Society of Dramatic Authors.

198. Rea, Charlotte. "Women for Women." Drama Review,
     18 (Dec. 1974), 77-87.

     Update of 1972 article (see below), with
     information on new women's theater groups.

199. _____. "Women's Theatre Groups." Drama Review,
     16 (June 1972), 79-89.

     Emphasizes performing collectives but also
     gives an account of the female playwrights of
     Westbeth Feminist Collective. Describes several
     of their plays and notes that the playwrights are
     "exploring the female consciousness in their
     scripts, trying to develop serious, three-
     dimensional roles for women."

200. Ross, David Allan. "Alice Seizes the Pencil."
     Independent Woman, 15 (Jan. 1936), 10-11,
     24-26.

     Praises the literary efforts of contemporary
     American women. There are "indications of
     debility among male authors," but women are writing
     important books. Their success is attributed to
     their "innate talents of observation, perception,
     and contemplation"; also, women's experiences are
     deeper and more enduring than those of men.

201. Sitwell, Osbert. "The Strong School of Women
Novelists." Saturday Review of Literature,
Dec. 8, 1934, p. 339. Discussion, Jan. 5,
1935, p. 414.

Attack on contemporary female novelists,
written in verse. Bemoans the "empty cradle" and
the "empty kitchen" and wishes "the tending of
living things/ Could soften your hardness."

Discussion - Verse making fun of Sitwell.

202. "Some 'Lady Novelists' and Their Works: As Seen
from a Public Library." Literary World,
June 3, 1882, pp. 184-186.

Discusses several works by popular female
novelists, such as Caroline Lee Hentz and Ann
Stephens. Advises libraries not to buy "trashy
and sensational" books by the "lady novelists."

203. Spacks, Patricia Meyer. "A Chronicle of Women."
Hudson Review, 25 (Spring 1972), 157-170.

Review of recent works by women. Says her
sampling affords a "consistent and depressing view
of the feminine psyche." Women writers seem to
lack self-knowledge. If there is any specifically
feminine characteristic in recent novels by women,
it is "the emotional equivalent and consequence of
centuries of social restriction, a special
atmosphere of resentment expressed and concealed
in many ways, emblem of the feminine condition,
both source and underminer of literary energy."

204. Tiger, Virginia. "Advertisements for Herself."
Columbia Forum, 3 (Spring 1974), 15-19.
Discussion, 3 (Summer 1974), inside cover and
p. 49.

Contends that recent novels by and about
women are confessional in nature. They examine
female protagonists' individual selves and show
less engagement than novels by men.

205. Trilling, Diana. "The Image of Women in
      Contemporary Literature." The Woman in
      America. Edited by Robert Jay Lifton.
      Boston: Houghton, Mifflin and Co., 1965.
      Pp. 52-71.

      Speech to a conference on the superior woman
student held at Columbia University, May 23, 1964.
The topic is "the influence of our contemporary
literary culture on the gifted young college
woman." Trilling complains that the women writers
of the 1950's and 1960's "echo the male voice" in
writing only of alienation and emptiness. Implicit
in the discussion is the premise that women should
be guardians of moral values.

206. "Twenty Immortelles." Critic, Aug. 30, 1890, p.
      108; Oct. 25, 1890, pp. 206-207; Dec. 27,
      1890, p. 342.

      Announcement, results, and analysis of
reader opinion poll. The stated object was to get
a consensus "as to the relative merits of
contemporaneous female writers." Interestingly
enough, however, the announcement asks readers to
vote for the 20 writers who are "the truest
representatives of what is best in cultivated
American womanhood." Harriet Beecher Stowe led
the poll.

207. Von Wien, Florence. "Playwrights Who Are Women."
      Independent Woman, 25 (Jan. 1946), 12-14.

      On contemporary American women playwrights.
Notes that there are few successful female
dramatists, but there is also a small number of
distinguished male playwrights. In the history of
the drama "the dramatists whose plays are worth
reviving are few and far between."

208. Walker, Cheryl. "Welcome Eumenides: Contemporary
      Feminist Poets." Feminist Art Journal, 2
      (Winter 1973-74), 6-7, 10.

      Discussion of feminist poets, such as Robin
Morgan and Adrienne Rich, in terms of Trotsky's
ideas on revolutionary art. Good feminist poetry
is "a poetry of risk" and never strictly
confessional; "it transforms the personal into
what Trotsky calls the 'super-personal,' which is
social revelation." Contemporary feminist poets

are performing the dual function of the
Eumenides--they are both avengers and protectors,
who lead us to wisdom through suffering.

209. Wasserman, Barbara Alson. "Introduction." The
        Bold New Women. Edited by Barbara Alson
        Wasserman. Greenwich, Conn.: Fawcett
        publications, 1970. (orig. pub. 1966)
        Pp. 9-11.

        Introduction to anthology of fiction and
poetry by contemporary women. Sees a change in
women's writing in the past few years; it is
"tougher, less sentimental, less euphemistic."
Female authors have been following their "natural
bent," which is "to write subjectively rather than
objectively, and to write about sex."

210. Wernick, Robert. "The Queens of Fiction." Life,
        Apr. 6, 1959, pp. 139-152.

        Discussion of the lives and works of 3
"queens" of bestsellerdom, Edna Ferber, Frances
Parkinson Keyes, and Taylor Caldwell. Claims that
the 3 writers share a knack for "striking
feminine portraits," a tendency to portray their
heroines dominating men, and an "intense nostalgia
for the American past."

211. Willson, Norma. "Majority Report: The New Women's
        Poetry." English Journal, 64 (Mar. 1975)
        26-28.

        Excerpts from recent poetry, arranged to form
an imaginary group discussion on contemporary
women's poetry. Emphasis is on the changing
consciousness of the female poet and her ability to
talk more openly about being female.

212. "Woman in the Domain of Letters." American
        Monthly Knickerbocker, 64 (July 1864), 83-86.

        Assessment of women's contribution to
literature. Believes women are now superior to men
in the field of "light literature" (i.e. fiction);
they excel in creation of character and exercise a
"refining, elevating influence" on literature.
Women do not "unsex" themselves in writing; the
question of women's sphere "settles itself: for the
inevitable test of sphere is success."

213. "Women and the American Theatre," <u>Nation</u>, June 1,
     1918, p. 665.

     Discussion of several contemporary women
     playwrights. While there are many eminent
     actresses, there are few female dramatists who
     deserve serious consideration. Female dramatists
     have two "great disabilities": a "limited outlook
     on life" (this is rapidly disappearing) and a lack
     of discipline and mastery of structure.

214. Zinnes, Harriet. "Seven Women Poets." <u>Carleton
     Miscellany</u>, 14, No. 2 (1974), 122-126.

     Review of recent poetry by women. Praises
     several poets but finds an "appalling despair" in
     the work of the younger women. Poets like Robin
     Morgan use a "rhetoric of hate" and reveal
     "infantile" attitudes. Women poets should write
     poetry, not polemics.

See also: 34, 40, 42, 47, 51, 59, 66, 73, 75, 77, 96,
           100, 110, 223, 230, 238, 245, 248, 267, 291,
           316

VI. FEMININE SENSIBILITY

215. Abbott, Lawrence F. "Sex in Art." Outlook,
        July 8, 1925, pp. 355-356.

        Ambivalent and often contradictory essay on
      women and poetry. Finds the terms "poetess" and
      "female poet" offensive because it is foolish to
      maintain any differentiation between the sexes in
      the creative arts. However, there is much truth
      in the idea that women ought not to write poetry;
      in having children a woman is doing the "greatest
      creative work in the world, from which she ought
      not to be diverted." Woman is capable of writing
      enduring poetry, though; that she has not done so
      is due to "the long centuries of suppression of
      her intellectual faculties." Ends by asking
      whether women's limitations are the surmountable
      ones of education and experience or the "inherent
      and immutable limitations of sex."

216. Adams, J. Donald. "Women and Fiction." American
        Mercury, 69 (Sept. 1949), 304-310. Also in
        Literary Frontiers. New York: Duell, Sloan
        and Pearce, 1951. Pp. 43-69.

        Discussion of female writers, readers, and
      fictional characters. Somewhat confusing, but
      interesting, in that almost every cliche about
      women writers which appears on one page is modified
      on another. Thus Adams states that women novelists
      differ from men novelists in their capacity for
      sympathy and preoccupation with personal relation-
      ships, yet later claims that it is difficult to
      distinguish the fiction of women and men. Female
      novelists are taken to task for not portraying male
      characters objectively, but men writers create
      unrealistic heroines, especially the "dream girl"
      or "the bitch."

217. Bogan, Louise. "Verse." New Yorker, Apr. 27, 1963, pp. 173-175.

Argues that "women's poetry continues to be unlike men's, all feminist statements to the contrary notwithstanding." Women cannot be "directly destructive" and cannot abandon reason; there are no "poetesses maudites" or female surrealists.

218. Brazelton, Ethel M. Colson. Writing and Editing for Women. New York: Funk & Wagnalls Co., 1927. 252pp.

Mainly advice for prospective women journalists and magazine writers; however, much commentary, especially in Chapters 1 and 9, on the differences between men's and women's writing. Women and men have "naturally diverging viewpoints." The special province of female creative writers is fiction for children, and women literary critics are best at reviewing fiction or "books addressed to the emotions."

219. Cestre, Charles. "Women and Obscenity." Saturday Review of Literature, Nov. 26, 1932, pp. 265-266.

Tries to explain why many of the "most daring sex novels" have been written by women. According to the "new science of physio-psychology," women are capable of both more passion and more self-composure than men. Women can experience passion and analyze it at the same time.

220. Clarke, Edith E. "Woman in Literature at the Fair, from the Standpoint of a Librarian and Cataloger." Library Journal, 19 (Feb. 1894) 47-49.

Discussion of the Women's Library, a collection of 7,000 books by women exhibited at the World's Fair in Chicago in 1893. Contends that a special exhibit was necessary to advertise women's accomplishments in literature; however, in general there should be no distinctions made between male and female authors, for "sex in literature does not exist."

221. Colum, Mary M. "The Woman-Artist." Forum, 92
     (Oct. 1934), 212-216. Discussion, 93 (Jan.
     1935), 64.

   Claims that "most women-writers and artists
   [are] second- or third-rate in comparison with
   men." The reason is their inability to push
   beyond their subjective personality to a "universal
   personality." The "intellectual and psychological
   freedom" required to make this step has been denied
   to women.

   Discussion - Considers social and economic factors
   of greater importance.

222. Coppée, Henry. "Introduction." A Gallery of
     Distinguished English and American Female
     Poets. Philadelphia: E. H. Butler & Co.,
     1860. Pp. xi-xxiii.

   Contains high praise for the poets included
   in the anthology. If there is a conceded place for
   women in the world of literature, it is in poetry.
   In poetry women are the equal of men, although
   their poetry is different. Women tend toward
   "spontaneous song," marked by intuition rather
   than intellect. The poetry of woman reveals her
   "particular moral beauty," which consists of
   "gratitude, charity, and faith."

223. Courtney, W. L. The Feminine Note in Fiction.
     London: Chapman & Hall, 1904. 276pp.

   Essays on English and American novelists,
   including Gertrude Atherton and Mary E. Wilkins
   Freeman. In his introduction Courtney claims that
   women have their own point of view and a
   "distinctive feminine style." They have a "passion
   for detail" and are too autobiographical and too
   didactic, being unable to "realize the neutrality
   of the artistic mind." Any women writers who seem
   to be exceptions to this rule are defined as
   masculine. Thus, George Eliot was "essentially a
   masculine genius, in no respect characteristically
   feminine. In other words, she was an artist--an
   ideal which the average female writer finds it
   difficult to attain."

224. Denne, Constance Ayers, and Rogers, Katharine M.
"On Women Writers." <u>Nation</u>, Aug. 30, 1975,
pp. 151-153.

Description of MLA panel discussion (see
below). Summarizes the views of the panelists and
concludes that women writers suffer doubly from
cultural bias. Their "distinctive subject matter"
is disparaged, yet they are attacked if they are
too "masculine." Freedom for the woman writer
means freedom "from anxiety about whether to
conform to a limiting feminine stereotype or be
condemned for invading masculine territory."
Hopefully, in the future women will be able to use
all experience and have no "self-consciousness of
being a separate group."

225. _____. "Women Novelists: A Distinct Group?"
<u>Women's Studies</u>, 3, No. 1 (1975), 5-28.

Important panel discussion at the December,
1974 Modern Language Association Convention, with
Elizabeth Hardwick, Erica Jong, Nancy Milford, and
Elaine Showalter. The principal question is
whether "woman writer" or "feminine consciousness"
can be defined. The panelists note that any
definition can be used to support harmful
stereotypes, but most believe there is some
tradition which unites women writers. Much of the
discussion involves the appropriation of female
experience by male writers; men feel they have a
right to the female consciousness, but they deny
women the right to tap male sensibility.

226. "Does 'The Woman Writer' Exist?" <u>Publisher's
Weekly</u>, Apr. 5, 1976, pp. 24-25.

Account of the Women Writers Symposium,
sponsored by Doubleday and held in New York on
March 16. Panelists Lois Gould, Jill Robinson,
Cynthia Ozick, Ellen Moers, and Muriel Rukeyser
debated the following questions: Does 'the woman
writer' exist? Is there a female language? In
writing from female experience, is it possible to
move from the particular to the universal? See
#233 for another account of the symposium.

227. Donovan, Josephine. "Feminist Style Criticism."
<u>Images of Women in Fiction: Feminist
Perspectives</u>. Edited by Susan Koppelman
Cornillon. Bowling Green, Ohio: Bowling Green

University Popular Press, 1972. Pp. 341-354.
Also in Female Studies VI: Closer to the
Ground: Women's Classes, Criticism, Programs--
1972. Edited by Nancy Hoffman, Cynthia Secor,
and Adrian Tinsley. Old Westbury, N. Y.:
Feminist Press, 1972. Pp. 139-149.

Asks whether there is such a thing as a female
prose style. Virginia Woolf and Dorothy Richardson
believed that there is, and they are corroborated
on many points by Nathalie Sarraute and Mary
Ellmann. Donovan defines a female prose style as
one which "enables the writer to deal with the
psychic, personal, emotional, 'inner' details of
life in a way that is neither analytic nor
authoritarian." She finds such a style in Woolf,
Richardson, and Kate Chopin and calls for close
stylistic analysis of an extensive number of works
by women writers in order to see if they share the
same traits.

228. Drew, Elizabeth A. "Is There a 'Feminine'
        Fiction?" The Modern Novel: Some Aspects of
        Contemporary Fiction. New York: Harcourt,
        Brace and Co., 1926. Pp. 103-116.

The answer is yes, because it is "absolutely
inherent in the nature of woman" that she is
dependent on personal relationships for her
happiness in the world. Women writers thus
emphasize relationships in their fiction. Drew
stresses the new freedom of the female writer--she
has "complete liberty of action . . . and speech."
However, "the creative genius of woman remains
narrower than that of man, even in the novel."

229. Farnham, Marynia F. "The Pen and the Distaff."
        Saturday Review of Literature, Feb. 22, 1947,
        pp. 7-8, 29-30. Discussion, Mar. 29, 1947,
        p. 19.

Attempt by psychiatrist to fit women writers
into her theory of femininity. "Women's area in
writing" is almost exclusively fiction, and female
fiction writers are almost exclusively concerned
with the "individualized man-woman relationship."
Uninterested in the larger world, women stress the
"intimate, personal, immediate, and intuitive."

230. "The Female Poets of America." United States
     Magazine and Democratic Review, 24 (Mar.
     1849), 232-241.

     Criticizes Griswold (#238) for implying that
     a poem should be judged according to the sex of its
     writer; there is no such thing as male poetry and
     female poetry. Professes to be "aghast at the
     numbers of the Female Poets" now writing in
     America, for most of their poetry is mediocre.

231. "Feminine Sensibility: A Forum." Harvard Advocate,
     106 (Winter 1973), 7-19.

     Responses of 20 women writers to Virginia
     Woolf's contention that the sensibility and
     creative power of women differs from that of men.
     A majority of the writers disagree with Woolf and
     see her as projecting her own sensibility and
     background.

232. Follett, Wilson. "The Printed Word; Altogether
     Feminine." Bookman, 70 (Nov. 1929), 285-288.

     Claims that "the celebrated quality of
     femininity in written style is almost strictly
     limited to punctuation." Women are addicted to
     gratuitous quotation marks, "ecstatic exclamation
     points," dashes, and underlining; thus they produce
     "the coo, the gurgle, the simper."

233. Friedrich, Molly. "Writing Hath No Sex,
     BUT . . . ." Majority Report, Apr. 17-May 1,
     1976, p. 9.

     Another account (see #226) of the Women
     Writers Symposium. The panelists debated the
     question of whether there is a "feminine
     sensibility" or uniquely female literary tradition.
     Cynthia Ozick stated that categorizing writers by
     sex is arbitrary and meaningless; the majority of
     the panelists and audience concurred, yet "never
     without a substantial 'but.'"

234. Getsi, Lucia. "Inventing Us: The Open Word."
     Mundus Artium, 7, No. 2 (1974), 7-9.

     Distinguishes between horizontal and vertical
     modes of perception, the former being concerned
     with the external world and the latter with inward

depths. Until very recently women writers were
limited to the vertical mode because they were not
allowed to function freely in the external world;
however, male critics used the horizontal mode of
perception to judge female writers. Now the vision
of women is spreading out and they are uniting the
vertical and the horizontal.

235. Gilbert, Sandra M. "Out of the Women's Museum."
     Poetry, 127 (Oct. 1975), 44-55.

     Review of several recent poetry books by
women. Asks whether gender makes a difference in
poetry and concludes that on the one hand art has
no sex; however, "what it means to be a woman poet
is tautological but significant: it means to be a
woman who is a poet," that is, a person who has
experienced discrimination.

236. Gill, Elaine. "Introduction." Mountain Moving
     Day: Poems by Women. Edited by Elaine Gill.
     Trumansburg, N. Y.: The Crossing Press, 1973.
     Pp. [7-8].

     Introduction to anthology of contemporary
poems. Emphasizes the range of poetry by women,
arguing that female poets do not have a narrower
range than male poets. Women's poetry has
"immense vitality" and differs widely in subject
and tone.

237. Green, Alice Stopford. "Woman's Place in the World
     of Letters." Nineteenth Century, 41 (June
     1897), 964-974. Also in Living Age, July 31,
     1897, pp. 300-307. Discussion, Spectator,
     June 5, 1897, pp. 796-797.

     Contends that "woman's place" is hard to
determine because of her mysteriousness. Women
writers fear to "venture out into the open
unprotected and bare to attack"; they are also
hostile to the past and write as though they were
strangers to the "history and philosophy of man."
The essay is full of abstraction and inflated
language.

Discussion - Criticizes the article for saying
little on the subject and instead painting woman as
a mystery.

238. Griswold, Rufus Wilmot. "Preface." The Female
     Poets of America. 2nd ed. Philadelphia:
     Henry C. Baird, 1852. (1st ed. 1848)
     Pp. 7-10.

     Argues that "it is less easy to be assured of
the genuineness of literary merit in women than in
men" because one may mistake the "exuberance of
personal feelings" for creative energy. The
"conditions of aesthetic ability" in the two sexes
are "distinct, or even opposite"; genius in men is
marked by feminine qualities, whereas the best
female poet is one whose "emotions are refined by
reason." Praises American women poets for having
reached as "high and sustained a range of poetic
art" as women of any age or country.

239. Grumbach, Doris. "On Women Novelists."
     Commonweal, May 8, 1964, pp. 198-200.
     Discussion, July 10, 1964, p. 484.

     Attack on women novelists. Women who write
are belittled, but the author shows hardly any
familiarity with past or present novels by women.
"No women have produced large-scale novels of any
great worth. Nor have they shown evidence of
being innovators in any way, either in style or
form." Women cannot handle allegory, parable,
science fiction, tragedy, social criticism, satire,
philosophical comment, or ideas in general; on the
"positive and hopeful" side, however, they have
written historical novels indistinguishable from
those of men.

240. Howe, Florence. "Introduction." No More Masks!
     An Anthology of Poems by Women. Edited by
     Florence Howe and Ellen Bass. Garden City,
     N. Y.: Anchor Books, 1973. Pp. 3-33.

     Introduction to anthology representing 87
modern American poets. Analyzes at length the
"changing sensibility" of female poets from the
1920's to the 1970's. Discusses several themes
which unify the poetry of women, with emphasis on
female sexuality, identity (especially "the divided
self or split woman"), and creativity. A
discussion of Black poets is included.

241.   Joad, Cyril M. "Complaint against Lady Novelists."
       New Statesman & Nation, Aug. 19, 1939,
       pp. 275-276. Discussion, Aug. 26, 1939,
       p. 311; Sept. 9, 1939, p. 375.

       Professes himself "naturally prejudiced
against lady novelists," and argues that they are
too concerned with analyzing personal
relationships. Their characters do not act and do
not think about the world.

Discussion - Naomi Mitchison strongly disagrees
and says of Joad's article, "It hurts"; male
respondant considers the statement "It hurts" a
"staggering" one because it is not "objective."

242.   Jones, W. A. "Female Novelists." United States
       Magazine and Democratic Review, 14 (May 1844),
       484-489.

       Praises the accomplishments of American,
English, and Swedish women novelists and attempts
to distinguish between the abilities of women and
men in writing fiction. Women excel at the novel
of manners and the sentimental novel; they are
more emotional and witty. Men reason better and
show more experience of the world, being able to
portray social classes other than their own.

243.   Jong, Erica. "Three Sisters." Parnassus, 1
       (1972), 77-88.

       Review of 3 new books by women poets.
Discusses at length the "special dimension we look
for in writing by women that cannot be present in
writing by men." As "the Other" in our culture,
women do not write with the certainty that they
are "natural inheritors of cultural tradition."
They are also treated as the Other by critics--
they are seldom taken seriously while they are
alive. Contends that the greatest artists of the
next generation will be Blacks and women; because
of their otherness, they will be able to "tap the
well-springs of the unconscious and deepest shared
fantasies of the human race."

244.   Juris, Prudence. "Excerpts from a Letter."
       Margins, No. 7 (Aug.-Sept. 1973), 5.

       Contends that women and men do not write
differently; critics should not stress gender.

245. Kazin, Alfred. "Cassandras." Bright Book of Life:
     American Novelists and Storytellers from
     Hemingway to Mailer. Boston: Little, Brown
     and Co., 1971. Pp. 165-205.

        Chapter on women writers from Katherine Anne
     Porter to Joyce Carol Oates. Good illustration of
     the politics which can be involved in the
     designation "women's fiction." To Kazin "'woman's
     fiction' exists not as writing by women but as
     inordinate defensiveness against a society
     conceived as the special enemy of the sensitive."
     Shirley Jackson writes "woman's fiction" because
     "woman as victim" is often the main figure; Oates
     writes something better than "woman's fiction"
     because "she is not concerned with demonstrating
     power relationships."

246. Matthews, Brander. "Women Dramatists." A Book
     about the Theater. New York: Charles
     Scribner's Sons, 1916. Pp. 113-125.

        Asks why there have been so few successful
     women dramatists. Female playwrights have equal
     opportunity with men, but women lack experience of
     life; they also have no "scientific imagination"
     and thus are "deficient in the faculty of
     construction." Female novelists are similarly
     handicapped, so that "no woman novelist is to be
     ranked among the supreme leaders."

247. May, Caroline. "Preface." Pearls from the
     American Female Poets. New York: Allen
     Brothers, 1869. Pp. v-viii.

        Notes that the number of female poets is
     especially large in America and the value of their
     works is often underrated. Because few women can
     escape domestic duties, their themes are often
     "derived from the incidents and associations of
     every-day life." Also, women's poems are emotional
     because their inspiration is from the heart rather
     than the head.

248. Mencken, H. L. "The Novel." Prejudices: Third
     Series. New York: Alfred A. Knopf, 1922.
     Pp. 201-212.

        Contends that women are writing novels as
     good as those by men and are "actually surpassing
     men in their experimental development of the novel

form." Women succeed at writing fiction because
they are better fitted than men for realistic
representation. "They see the facts of life more
sharply and are less distracted by mooney dreams.
Women seldom have the pathological faculty vaguely
called imagination."

249.   Mersand, Joseph. When Ladies Write Plays: An
          Evaluation of Their Contributions to the
          American Drama. The Modern Woman Chapbooks,
          No. 2. New York: The Modern Chapbooks, 1937.
          25 pp. Also in Players Magazine, 14 (Sept.
          1937), 7-8, 26, 28. Also in The American
          Drama 1930-1940: Essays on Playwrights and
          Plays. Freeport, N. Y.: Books for Libraries
          Press, 1971. (1st pub. 1941) Pp. 145-161.
          Also in The American Drama Since 1930: Essays.
          Port Washington, N. Y.: Kennikat Press, 1968.
          (1st pub. 1949) Pp. 149-166.

        Claims that the twentieth century marks "the
brilliant efflorescence of women as creative
dramatists." However, most of the essay is an
attack on female dramatists. Women's
"preoccupation with the commonplace" and ability
to "recall details with remarkable accuracy" makes
them specialists in realistic drama. They do not
write "great drama": they are weak in poetic drama
and fail to elicit strong emotional response or
climb to "ethereal heights."

250.   Milburn, William Henry. "An Hour's Talk about
          Woman." The Rifle, Axe, and Saddle-Bags, and
          Other Lectures. New York: Derby & Jackson,
          1857. Pp. 137-209.

        Defines "women's sphere" as literature as well
as the home and thus discusses women's accomplishments in literature and motives for writing.
Female authors write because they cannot help it;
they need to "unburden their hearts." They are
lacking in genius and experience, but their "deep
and gentle sensibility" makes up for any
deficiencies. Women are especially fitted to
create literature for their own sex and for
children.

251. Miles, Rosalind. The Fiction of Sex: Themes and
     Functions of Sex Difference in the Modern
     Novel. New York: Barnes & Noble, 1974.
     208pp.

     Contends that critics should not distinguish
     between male and female writers because works by
     women are thereby confined to a "pejorative
     subsection of literature." It has never been
     shown that creative men and women think or write
     differently or that women writers have anything in
     common as a group. Some provocative arguments, but
     the author often contradicts her own thesis. For
     instance, she claims on the one hand that there
     is no female tradition in novel writing and on the
     other hand that the feminine subjective novelistic
     tradition is damaging to women's interests because
     it portrays women as separate and different from
     men.

252. Moore, Virginia. "Women Poets." Bookman, 71
     (July 1930), 388-395.

     Survey of the accomplishments of women poets.
     Stresses differences between female and male poets
     and claims that women have been "highly deficient
     in the distinguishing talents of the great poets."
     Women lack dramatic, philosophic, and epic talents
     and "neglect the cosmos." They are more emotional
     and spontaneous than men and thus tend to be
     lyricists. Female poets will some day "grow to
     the epic-making stature."

253. Ozick, Cynthia. "Women and Creativity: The Demise
     of the Dancing Dog." Motive, 29 (Mar.-Apr.
     1969), 7-16. Also in Woman in Sexist Society:
     Studies in Power and Powerlessness. Edited by
     Vivian Gornick and Barbara K. Moran. New
     York: Basic Books, Inc., 1971. Pp. 431-451.

     Describes the author's encounters with the
     "Ovarian Theory of Literature." When she taught
     at a university she found that her students and
     colleagues all distinguished between men's and
     women's writing, as if people wrote with their sex
     organs. The prevailing myths damn women from every
     direction--for instance, she is too sensitive and
     emotional to be president of General Motors and not
     sensitive and emotional enough to write King Lear.
     Witty essay, but elitist in outlook. Most people
     are "mediocre"; students are "alike in illiteracy,
     undereducation, ignorance, and prejudice."

254. Peckham, H. Houston. "The New Feminism in
        Literature." South Atlantic Quarterly, 14
        (Jan. 1915), 68-74.

        Notes the increased literary activity of
    American women and concludes that the "new
    feminist movement" may lead to "the emancipation
    of literature from the crudeness of masculinity."
    Because women are naturally more artistic and less
    scientific than men, the time may come when
    "literature will be considered as peculiarly a
    woman's function."

255. "Phrases of the Feminine Fictionist." Living Age,
        May 20, 1911, pp. 509-510.

        Satirizes female authors, claiming that
    fiction by women is full of words and phrases
    "used and understood by women alone." For
    instance, "man-like," "alright," "dainty,"
    "horrid," "ripple" (instead of "laugh"), and
    "flash" (instead of "reply") are women's words.
    The implication is that women's style is affected
    and over-emotional.

256. "Preface." Selections from Female Poets: A Present
        for Ladies. Boston: Samuel Colman, 1837.
        Pp. iii-iv.

        Claims to be the first anthology of poetry
    exclusively by women and notes that "the line of
    distinction between male and female writers is
    sufficiently definite and broad to render their
    separate classification a matter of propriety and
    advantage." Discerns a "feminine cast of thought
    and style" in the poems but does not specify what
    it is.

257. Review of The Female Prose Writers of America, by
        John S. Hart. Southern Quarterly Review,
        N. S. 5 (1852), 114-121.

        Takes up the question of whether woman may
    write "without injury to her strictly domestic
    attributes." She can, to a limited extent,
    especially since "there is in literature a sphere
    peculiarly woman's." This sphere is "light"
    literature which impresses upon young girls "the
    part they must play in life." The purity of the
    female mind makes her writing an "instrument for
    the quieting of passion and disarming of vice."

258. Review of <u>Hope</u> <u>Leslie</u>, or <u>Early</u> <u>Times</u> <u>in</u>
     <u>Massachusetts</u>, by "the author of 'Redwood.'"
     <u>North</u> <u>American</u> <u>Review</u>, 26 (Apr. 1828),
     403-420.

          General discussion of "female literature."
     Literature by women is "peculiar in its nature and
     distinct in its influence." Women are best
     qualified to write books for juveniles and "light"
     literature (fiction and poetry). The female
     influence has been "powerful and good," purifying
     the morals of literature and establishing a code
     of decency.

259. Richart, Bette. "Since Sappho." Review of <u>The</u>
     <u>Unicorn</u> <u>and</u> <u>Other</u> <u>Poems</u>, by Anne Morrow
     Lindbergh. <u>Commonweal</u>, Sept. 7, 1956,
     pp. 568-570. Discussion, Oct. 12, 1956,
     pp. 48-49.

          Focuses on the "polite tradition of women
     writing for women," of which Lindbergh's book is a
     product. Claims that there have been no great
     women poets and few good ones since Sappho. Women
     are incapable of wit and tragedy and too "gentle"
     and "lady-like" to write good poetry.

     Discussion - Josephine Jacobsen quotes from
     several contemporary women poets whom she considers
     "good, unladylike poets."

260. Rizza, Peggy. "Another Side of This Life: Women
     as Poets." <u>American</u> <u>Poetry</u> <u>Since</u> <u>1960</u>: <u>Some</u>
     <u>Critical</u> <u>Perspectives</u>. Edited by Robert B.
     Shaw. Chester Springs, Pa.: Dufour Editions,
     1974. Pp. 167-179.

          Considers to what extent the feminine stereo-
     types of formlessness, hysteria, and confinement
     (see Ellmann, #327) are found in the poetry of
     Elizabeth Bishop, Anne Sexton, Maxine Kumin, and
     Mona Van Duyn. Concludes that the poets have been
     affected more by contemporary tastes in poetry
     (for instance, "autobiography, confessionalism,
     and formal elegance") than by sexual stereotypes
     or their own "sexual self-concepts." It is no
     easier to find characteristics common to female
     poets than for any random group of poets.

261. Robinson, Lillian S. "Who's Afraid of a Room of
     One's Own?" The Politics of Literature:
     Dissenting Essays on the Teaching of English.
     Edited by Louis Kampf and Paul Lauter. New
     York: Vintage Books, 1973. (1st pub. 1972)
     Pp. 354-411.

     Claims that the cultural condition of women
has not changed substantially since Virginia Woolf
wrote her feminist essay. However, unlike Woolf,
modern feminists have a strategy for change and
see the possibility of collective social action.
Makes many generalizations about women's fiction:
women have rarely constructed realistic male
characters; they dwell on superficial details of
dress and appearance; they tend to make
relationships between the sexes their principal
subject. The latter two characteristics are seen
as a result of the "sexualization of women's whole
life and psychology," the refusal of society to
allow women to transcend their sexual identities.

262. Routh, James. "Do Women Writers Use More Words
     per Idea than Men?" Journal of English and
     German Philology, 34 (Apr. 1935), 238-242.

     In scanning 49 specimens of prose, fiction and
non-fiction, the author counted the "strong" words,
"key words, or words bearing some unmistakable
sentence accent." He found that 61% of the living
male writers but only 35% of the living female
writers used a "strong style," that is, were above
the mean for strong words.

263. Ruby, Kathryn. "The Feminist Aesthetic: New
     Avenues." Margins, No. 7 (Aug.-Sept. 1973),
     3.

     Notes that the works of recent women poets
show a "definite feminist sensibility" and
attempts to define a feminist work.

264. _____. "Preface." We Become New: Poems by
     Contemporary American Women. Edited by
     Lucille Iverson and Kathryn Ruby. New York:
     Bantam Books, 1975. Pp. xii-xvii.

     Introduction to anthology of feminist poetry.
Discusses the need for collections of poetry and
fiction by women and considers "ways in which
women's writings constitute a distinctive literary

unit." Asks whether there is an "overall women's aesthetic" and gives arguments on both sides of the question.

265. Schulman, L. M. "Foreword." A Woman's Place: An Anthology of Short Stories. Edited by L. M. Schulman. New York: Macmillan Publishing Co., 1974. Pp. vii-ix.

Believes that the stories in the anthology "give the lie to stereotypes of 'women's writing.'" They are neither poetic nor sentimental nor vague. However, no man could have written them because no man could conceive of the "special agonies of an existence" without the rights he takes for granted.

266. Seawell, Molly Elliot. "On the Absence of the Creative Faculty in Women." Critic, Nov. 29, 1891, pp. 292-294. Discussion, Dec. 26, 1891, pp. 374-375; Jan. 16, 1892, pp. 41-42; Jan. 23, 1892, pp. 55-56; Feb. 6, 1892, pp. 89-90; Feb. 20, 1892, pp. 117-118; Feb. 27, 1892, pp. 132-133; Mar. 19, 1892, pp. 172-174; Apr. 23, 1892, p. 241; July 16, 1892, pp. 35-36; Aug. 20, 1892, p. 95; Aug. 27, 1892, p. 112.

Claims that "all men possess genius in some form, and no woman ever possessed it in any form"; women have never created anything important or lasting. The thesis is apparently intended to cover all forms of artistic creation, but in attempt to support it the author turns to women writers. Some writers might be considered exceptions, but they have not endured. If Sappho's poetry had really been great, it would have come down to us intact. Jane Austen is no exception because she "described," rather than created.

Discussion - Numerous letters, most calling the article "foolish" and "ignorant" and providing counterexamples. There are no less than 3 rebuttals by Seawell. The editors of Critic also reprint comments from newspapers and provide a running commentary on the controversy. They note that the article has been more criticized than any other single article ever published in Critic; however, they insist that none of Seawell's critics have proved her position untenable.

267.   Segnitz, Barbara, and Rainey, Carol.
       "Introduction." Psyche: The Feminine Poetic
       Consciousness. Edited by Barbara Segnitz and
       Carol Rainey. New York: Dial Press, 1973.
       Pp. 15-34.

       Introduction to anthology of poems by American
       women. Notes that women's roles have been narrowly
       defined and "the dominant idea unifying the poetry
       of women is that of defining, or more precisely
       redefining, themselves and their world more
       realistically." One group of female poets is
       subjective, beginning redefinition with the self;
       the other group is impersonal and concerned with
       mind, redefining through language. In the past
       female poets have been "very private and concerned
       with a small radius of existence." However, recent
       poets tend to speak out and are more direct in
       subject matter and tone.

268.   Simpson, Joan Murray. "Foreword." Without Adam:
       The Femina Anthology of Poetry. Edited by
       Joan Murray Simpson. London: Femina Books
       Ltd., 1968. Pp. 17-18.

       Introduction to anthology of poetry by
       American and English women. Says there are no
       "poetesses" represented; poets who are women resent
       this label because it is condescending. Nor are
       the poems "specifically feminine in outlook"
       because "there is no artificial division between
       men and women where the art of poetry is
       concerned."

269.   Smith, Lewis Worthington. "Introduction." Women's
       Poetry Today. Edited by Lewis Worthington
       Smith and Alice Carey Weitz. New York:
       George Sully & Co., 1929. Pp. v-xx.

       Introduction to anthology of poetry by women
       living at the time. Sixty-seven poets are
       represented, and there are short biographical
       sketches on each. The editors' purpose is to see
       if poetry by women reveals any "individual
       peculiarities of her nature." Smith fears that
       women, because they are physically weaker than men,
       are more in danger of being "tremulous rather than
       vibrant"; he sees an excess of "fugitive emotion"
       in the poetry. However, he applauds the fact that
       more women are writing poetry and gives figures to
       show the steady increase in the percentage of women
       represented in anthologies of American verse.

270. Spacks, Patricia Meyer. The Female Imagination.
        New York: Alfred A. Knopf, 1975. 326pp.

        Wide-ranging study of American and English
women writers and their fictional heroines. "A
special female self-awareness emerges through
literature in every period; women use their
creativity to reveal and combat their restricted
situation as women." The approach is thematic,
rather than historical, with chapters on "Power
and Passivity," "The Adolescent as Heroine," etc.
One innovation is the inclusion of comments by
students who took the author's course on women
writers. Spacks is usually patronizing toward
student comments, however; she does not apply to
her own writing the insights she makes in her
excellent first chapter. This chapter treats
problems of style, tone, and rhetorical stance in
criticism by women: Virginia Woolf evades her own
anger, Simone De Beauvoir strains for masculine
authority and reveals self-doubt, Mary Ellmann
is evasive, Kate Millett's commitment to anger
leads her to a muddled style.

271. Stratton, George Malcolm. "Woman's Mastery of the
        Story." Atlantic Monthly, 117 (May 1916),
        668-676.

        Argues that women have been successful at
writing fiction because they are naturally more
mobile in their feelings, more sympathetic, and
more passive than men; the "currents of female
imagination have their source in deeper recesses
of the mind." Nature gives genius more often to
men, but women as a group may soon excel men in
writing fiction.

272. "Tells by Its Color Whether a Poem Is Masculine or
        Feminine." Current Opinion, 62 (May 1917),
        358.

        Explains the theory of Reginald Wright
Kauffman that every poem evokes a color which is
inherent in the poem itself. Men's poems evoke
red, green, blue and indigo and women's orange,
yellow and violet. The best poems are brown,
which involves crossing the first masculine color
with "the merely secondary feminine."

273. Van Doren, Mark. "Women as Poets." <u>Nation</u>,
      Apr. 26, 1922, pp. 498-499.

          Review of several new books of poetry by
      women. Claims that grouping female poets together
      does not imply condescension or mere curiosity
      about women's contributions to the arts. Instead
      it shows "conviction that there is such a thing as
      woman's poetry, that women write differently from
      men just as they speak differently from men."

274. "Will Women Write the Great Novels of the Future?"
      <u>Current Opinion</u>, 60 (June 1916), 429-430.

          Summarizes George Malcolm Stratton's "Woman's
      Mastery of the Story" (#271) and concludes that
      women may be the great novelists of the future.

275. "Women and Bad Books." <u>Independent</u>, Nov. 21, 1907,
      pp. 1260-1261.

          Denies the current charge that female writers
      are responsible for an alleged lowering of the
      moral tone of literature. The charge is ironic
      because women are at the same time denounced for
      imposing "their own narrow standards of propriety"
      upon literature. Notes that the few women who
      have written "sensual fiction" portray passion
      from the masculine viewpoint; also female novelists
      draw male characters more accurately than male
      novelists do female characters. Perhaps women
      have "deeper insight and sympathy for an alien
      personality."

276. "Women Playwrights--A Symposium." <u>Books Abroad</u>,
      22 (Winter 1948), 16-21.

          Twenty leading playwrights and critics respond
      to the editors' query concerning women playwrights:
      why have they been less successful as dramatists
      than men? Answers range from denial of the premise
      to assertion that women cannot succeed at any art.
      Some respondants point out that women are
      comparative newcomers to play writing and male

producers are often prejudiced; others claim that
women are too subjective and lack the ability to
organize.

See also: 4, 14, 26, 51, 53, 63, 64, 68, 82, 93, 95,
102, 103, 104, 110, 116, 119, 127, 128, 133,
134, 149, 156, 162, 163, 165, 172, 175, 178,
182, 188, 189, 190, 191, 192, 197, 200, 203,
209, 211, 212, 213, 280, 284, 314, 317, 319,
320, 322, 327, 330, 334, 336, 360, 379, 383,
393, 402

VII. PROBLEMS

277. Bowen, Catherine Drinker. "We've Never Asked a
      Woman Before." Atlantic Monthly, 225 (Mar.
      1970), 82-86.

          Says the contemporary women's movement affects
      women writers profoundly, in giving them a clearer
      view of their capabilities. Women are learning
      that in a conflict between home and profession,
      the profession must not come second. Includes
      account of her personal experiences with
      discrimination.

278. Boyd, Susan Kuehn. "Authoress in an Apron."
      Writer, 72 (Oct. 1959), 15-17.

          Considers writing the most feasible of the
      arts for a housewife to follow. However, keeping
      house and writing is still a difficult combination
      because of the lack of quiet and time. Discusses
      various writing schedules and advises perseverance.

279. Cahill, Susan. "Introduction." Women and Fiction:
      Short Stories by and about Women. Edited by
      Susan Cahill. New York: New American Library,
      1975. Pp. xi-xix.

          Notes that women writers have lived and
      written in "varied and multiple environments."
      Many of the difficulties they have encountered,
      such as role conflict, prejudice, and lack of a
      room of their own, may have proved to be
      advantages. The "necessity of living in many
      worlds at once" may have disciplined women so as
      to enrich their writing.

280. Calisher, Hortense. "Women Re Women: No Important
      Woman Writer, I Think, Has Really Wanted to
      Write 'Like a Man.' They Had Too Much Taste."
      Mademoiselle, 70 (Feb. 1970), 188-189, 271-
      272, 274. Also in Women's Liberation and

<u>Literature</u>. Edited by Elaine Showalter. New York: Harcourt Brace Jovanovitch, 1971. Pp. 223-230.

Subtitle is a sentence from the article but not the main thesis. Calisher outlines negative attitudes toward women writers in the first half of this century and argues that many writers, such as Katherine Anne Porter, Carson McCullers, and Mary McCarthy, reacted by assuming a neutral voice and ignoring whole areas of their female sensibility and experience; their work was thereby damaged.

281. Chester, Laura, and Barba, Sharon. "From the Editors." <u>Rising Tides: 20th Century American Poets</u>. Edited by Laura Chester and Sharon Barba. New York: Washington Square Press, 1973. Pp. xxiii-xxvii.

Introduction to anthology. Discusses prejudice against women writers and traces the increase in the number of good women poets in this century to the improvement of women's condition in general. Anthology includes portraits and short biographies of the poets.

282. Cone, Helen Gray. "Woman in American Literature." <u>Century Magazine</u>, 40 (Oct. 1890), 921-930. Also in <u>Woman's Work in America</u> as "Woman in Literature." Edited by Annie Nathan Meyer. New York: Henry Holt and Co., 1891. Pp. 107-127.

Historical survey of women's contributions to American literature, with attention to the special problems they faced. Contends that women were "at a disadvantage both in production and in the disposal of the product"; they were often poorly educated, plagued by feelings of inferiority, and victimized by the "suave and chivalrous critic." However, women have "steadily gained in art" and should advance more rapidly with the advent of higher education for women.

283. Cornillon, Susan Koppelman. "The Fiction of Fiction." <u>Images of Women in Fiction: Feminist Perspectives</u>. Edited by Susan

Koppelman Cornillon. Bowling Green, Ohio:
Bowling Green University Popular Press, 1972.
Pp. 113-130.

Contends that most women novelists "reinforce
female shame by not discussing women's deviation
from the cultural myths of what is supposed to be
feminine." They fail to perceive themselves as
members of an oppressed group, identify with men,
and thus portray women as men see them, not as they
really are. Most tragic is the case of women who
do not write at all because they fear their
experiences are "unfeminine" and "unnatural."

284. Donnelly, Lucy Martin. "Poet and Feminist." New
      Republic, Apr. 29, 1916, pp. 337-339.

Claims that women have not distinguished
themselves in either verse or prose. However,
today "a serpent has whispered in the feminist's
ear the wisdom that poetic creation has ever been
a matter not of sex but of circumstance."
According to the feminist view, poetry has been
produced almost exclusively by middle-class men,
men who were inspired by women and aided by women's
domestic service. If the situation were reversed,
however, it is unclear whether women possess the
requisite "poetical patience" and "will to work
for the impersonal ends of art."

285. Fishel, Elizabeth. "Women's Fiction: Who's Afraid
      of Virginia Woolf?" Ramparts, 11 (June 1973),
      45-48.

Notes that there are fewer feminist novels
than feminist social critiques and reviews the
social and economic conditions which still prevent
women from writing fiction. Discusses women's
battles against the male publishing elite and the
efforts of Aphra, the feminist literary journal,
to provide an outlet for contemporary women
writers. The 1970's could be the beginning of a
renaissance in women's fiction, but feminist
writers will have to find "a voice that will blend
feminist politics and artistry."

286. Goulianos, Joan. "Women and the Avant-Garde
      Theater: Interviews with Rochelle Owens,
      Crystal Field, Rosalyn Drexler."
      Massachusetts Review, 13 (Winter/Spring 1972),
      257-267. Also Woman: An Issue. Edited by

Lee R. Edwards, Mary Heath and Lisa Baskin.
Boston: Little, Brown and Co., 1972. Pp. 257-
267.

Interviews with 2 playwrights and a director.
The discussion is focused on their experiences in
the theater specifically as women and on
discrimination against female playwrights.

287. Griffin, Susan; Leistiko, Norma; Shange, Ntozake;
and Schapiro, Miriam. "Women and the Creative
Process: A Discussion." Mosaic, 8
(Fall 1974), 91-118.

Panel discussion from symposium on "The
Creative Process in Literature and the Arts" held
at Stanford University Nov. 11-18, 1973. Griffin
and Shange discuss problems of women writers.
Griffin stresses the difficulties of combining
writing and childcare and of trying to express
women's real experiences, which are seldom
reflected or talked about. Shange relates the
struggles of Third World women writers, especially
their fear of being thought "smarter than men" and
paying a price for success. She believes women
are alienated from their bodies and wants to
develop "3rd World women's pornography."

288. Harland, Marion. "Domestic Infelicity of Literary
Women." Arena, 2 (Aug. 1890), 313-320.
Discussion, Spectator, Aug. 23, 1890, pp. 240-
241.

Discussion of difficulties faced by female
authors who are married. Although many literary
women are excellent homemakers, others must
struggle between "duty and genius." Husbands are
often exacting and when their wives become
successful writers try to restrain them out of
"envy and spite."

Discussion - British critic says husbands are not
adverse to their wives' practice of literature so
long as domestic duties are not neglected.

289. Hatterer, Lawrence J. "The Woman Artist." The
Artist in Society: Problems and Treatment of

the Creative Personality. New York: Grove
Press, 1965. Pp. 172-178.

Psychiatrist contends that "women creators
have very special problems." They are viewed with
suspicion and do not receive the support and
approval which are necessary for the artist. They
earn less than men and their works are often judged
according to stereotypes of feminine nature.
Hatterer indulges in some stereotyping of his own,
however. A woman must not be too aggressive in
trying to overcome these problems or she might
"lose her femininity"; she can marry a sympathetic
man, but men who support their wives' creative
efforts "are often dependent, passive personalities
or have male identity problems."

290. Howell, Barbara. "Diaries of Some Non-Mad
      Housewives." Writer's Digest, 55 (Feb. 1975)
      13-15.

Account of her interviews with contemporary
women writers with children. Before the interviews
she assumed it was a struggle for a woman to be a
writer and mother simultaneously. Now she
believes there is a "less publicized variety of the
woman writer--the joyful person whose life is
filled with lovers, children, country estates,
fame, money and laughter." She is closer to
reality than the Woolf-Plath-Fitzgerald legends.

291. Jennings, Carol. "The Woman Poet." New York
      Quarterly, 2 (Fall 1972), 112-130.

Considers several obstacles confronted by the
woman poet, especially the "problem of the
attitudes of the male-dominated society toward the
woman writer." Poetry by women is seldom well-
received and the common belief that male experience
is more worthwhile than female experience makes it
difficult for female poets to identify and adhere
to their own subject matter. Includes an
historical survey of women's poetry and a
discussion of those contemporary women poets who
write "with a strong sexual identity."

292. Johnson, Pamela Hansford. "If She Writes, Must She Be a Lady?" New York Times Book Review, Dec. 31, 1961, pp. 1, 22.

Objects to the term "lady novelist" as one more instance of discrimination against women writers. Also discusses other problems encountered by female writers--for instance, domestic interruptions and limited knowledge of industry and technology.

293. Jong, Erica. "The Artist as Housewife." Ms., 1 (Dec. 1972), 64-66, 100-106. Also in The First Ms. Reader. New York: Warner Paperback Library, 1973. Pp. 111-122.

Argues that it is harder for women than for men to become artists because women in our society have greater difficulty achieving selfhood--becoming independent, finding and trusting their own inner voice. Women often do not finish their written works because they fear success, which means failure as a woman. Exhorts women to write about being female, even though they must pay for it in disparaging reviews and a lower literary reputation.

294. Kenney, Susan M. "A Room of One's Own Revisited." University of Michigan Papers in Women's Studies, 1 (June 1974), 97-109.

Personal essay which imitates Virginia Woolf's style. Points out numerous exceptions to the often stated "fact" that great women writers have been childless. Creativity and maternity should not be considered mutually exclusive.

295. Killoh, Ellen Peck. "The Woman Writer and the Element of Destruction." College English, 34 (Oct. 1972), 31-38.

Discusses psychoanalyst Otto Rank's contention that women cannot be great artists because to create it is necessary to destroy and women cannot destroy. Rank was influenced by the stereotype of the "preserving" woman, but it becomes true when "we are alienated from our own angers and hostilities by childhood conditioning and by the requirements of adult female roles." This source of power should be available for the woman writer's conscious use. Takes Anais Nin as

an example of a woman writer whose art is damaged
by her inability to face her own anger.

296. Levin, Harry. "Janes and Emilies, or the Novelist
      as Heroine." Refractions: Essays in
      Comparative Literature. New York: Oxford
      University Press, 1966. Pp. 250-270.

      Takes issue with Simone de Beauvoir and
Virginia Woolf on the question of the limitations
placed on the woman writer. "If the field of the
woman writer has too long been circumscribed by
her role in society, it has been enlarged by her
emancipation during the modern epoch." Also,
"woman--never completely at a loss for words--has
never been at a great disadvantage as a story-
teller."

297. Lincoln, Victoria. "For Married Women Only."
      Writer, 69 (Oct. 1956), 304-306.

      Considers problems of the married woman
writer. "It all boils down to this: there is no
time in the life of a woman writer when she
couldn't use a good wife." Concludes, however,
that the married woman writer is lucky to be "at
the living center of her family" and has "the best
of two worlds."

298. _____. "Yes, Very Interesting." Harper's, 194
      (May 1947), 433-435.

      Very light article on social prejudice against
women who write. Assures the reader that women
writers make good wives and mothers.

299. "The Literary Lady." The Genteel Female: An
      Anthology. Edited by Clifton Joseph Furness.
      New York: Alfred A. Knopf, 1931. Pp. 256-266.

      Excerpts from nineteenth-century essays on
female authorship. There is a brief introduction
by Furness on the subject of prejudice against
women's writing. He says it "began in a colonial
narrowness of mind" and lingered through the
nineteenth century. An example is the case of
Harriet Beecher Stowe, who was accused of
neglecting her family for her writing.

300. Marple, Allen. "Off the Cuff." Writer, 76 (June
     1963), 5-6.

     Quotes and comments upon a letter from an
aspiring writer. She complains of the "Dr. Jekyll
and Mr. Hyde existence" of women writers who also
do housework and care for children.

301. Nin, Anais. "On Feminism and Creation." Michigan
     Quarterly Review, 13 (Winter 1974), 4-13.

     Discussion of "women's greater difficulties
in the world of creation." Women's self-confidence
has been damaged, and they often feel guilty and
anxious about writing. The solution is for women
to embark on an inner journey to restore their
confidence and self-image.

302. Olsen, Tillie. "Silences: When Writers Don't
     Write." Harper's, 231 (Oct. 1965), 153-161.
     Also in Images of Women in Fiction: Feminist
     Perspectives. Edited by Susan Koppelman
     Cornillon. Bowling Green, Ohio: Bowling Green
     University Popular Press, 1972. Pp. 97-112.
     Also in This Is Women's Work: An Anthology of
     Prose and Poetry. Edited by Susan Efros.
     San Francisco: Panjandrum Press, 1974.
     Pp. 1-18.

     Discussion of the influences which keep
writers from writing. Women are affected more than
men because they are trained to subordinate their
needs to others'. Of the women who have created
enduring literature, few have married and fewer
still have had children; motherhood is "almost
certain death to creation." Includes an account
of the author's personal silences due to family
and work responsibilities.

303. _____. "Women Who Are Writers in Our Century:
     One Out of Twelve." College English, 34
     (Oct. 1972), 6-17.

     Same theme as earlier article. According to
the author's sampling, one book is written by a
woman to four by men. But in terms of recognized
achievement, measured by use as texts, critical
reviews, etc., the ratio is approximately one
woman to twelve men. One reason is that "the
leeching of belief, of will; the damaging of
capacity" begins early for women--they lose will

and confidence. Other contributing factors are the
pressures of motherhood, devaluation of women
writers by critics, censorship, and self-censorship. Criticizes Calisher (#280) for advising
·women not to strain toward "world sensibility";
that is as natural to women as to men.

304. Piercy, Marge. "Books for the Daughters."
       Margins, No. 7 (Aug.-Sept. 1973), 1-2.

       Describes the consequences of women writing
especially for women. It is more difficult to get
published and reviewed and to win grants or prizes.
However, on the positive side, the woman writer
can get in touch with herself and with audiences
who care.

305. Rich, Adrienne. "When We Dead Awaken: Writing as
       Re-Vision." College English, 34 (Oct. 1972),
       18-25.

       Wide-ranging essay on the problems of women
trying to write in a male-controlled culture and
faced constantly by the "specter of male judgment."
"No male writer has written primarily or even
largely for women, or with the sense of women's
criticism as a consideration when he chooses his
materials, his theme, his language." But "every
woman writer has written for men even when . . .
she was supposed to be addressing women."
Hopefully this imbalance can change. Women writers
are awakening and searching for language and images
to express their new consciousness. Includes
autobiographical material.

306. Rodgers, Mary Augusta. "Housewife with an Office."
       Writer, 73 (Mar. 1960), 17-18.

       Discusses the difficulties involved in a
housewife's trying to write at home and recounts
the advantages of having an office.

307. Rogers, Alice. "The Literary Life of Woman: Does
       It Interfere with Her Domestic Life?"
       Outlook, Oct. 26, 1895, pp. 666-667.

       Yes--"she cannot combine the two." The
average woman of ordinary strength either ruins her
health trying to combine two careers or neglects

her domestic duties. If a woman marries and has
a family, she must make her literary life
subsidiary.

308. Rogers, Alma A. "The Absence of Woman in
        Literature." Arena, 30 (Nov. 1903), 510-516.

        Seeks the cause of "woman's inferior status
in literature" and concludes that "in becoming the
mother of the race, woman has used those forces
which in man have sought expression in forms of
art." Believes women have developed their emotions
at the expense of intellect and exhorts female
authors to "learn to think."

309. Russ, Joanna. "What Can a Heroine Do? Or Why
        Women Can't Write." Images of Women in
        Fiction: Feminist Perspectives. Edited by
        Susan Koppelman Cornillon. Bowling Green,
        Ohio: Bowling Green University Popular Press,
        1972. Pp. 3-20.

        Argues that women writers are handicapped
because our culture is male and "our literary myths
are for heroes, not heroines." There are few plot-
patterns available for the female protagonist--she
cannot be the tough Western hero or private eye,
the "Romantic Poet Glamorously Doomed," the "Crass
Businessman," etc. Women writers can restrict
themselves to male myths with male protagonists,
but then they falsify their own experiences.
Hopefully, women can exploit the possibilities of
the "lyric mode," which does not depend on plot,
and begin to create their own myths.

310. Schroeder, Robert. "Symposium: The Woman
        Playwright." Dramatists Guild Quarterly,
        9 (Spring 1972), 45-47.

        Account of the Dramatists Guild's Symposium
on the Woman Playwright, held on Feb. 3. Most of
the symposium seems to have had nothing to do with
the topic, as panelist June Havoc discusses pass-
port problems and moderator Howard Teichmann
describes his fist fight with a director. However,
Havoc does say, "It is hell to be a woman and a
writer." Panelist Joan Rivers disagrees, claiming
that the woman writer is comparatively well-
treated in the theater; she can get her way by
crying and can gain sympathy if she is pregnant.

311. Showalter, Elaine. "Killing the Angel in the
      House: The Autonomy of Women Writers."
      Antioch Review, 32, No. 3 (1973), 339-353.

      Criticizes Virginia Woolf's theory of the
superiority of androgynous writing, writing which
"transcends consciousness of sex." The androgyny
theory "represents an escape from the confrontation
with femininity." Like the "Angel in the House,"
Woolf's name for the specter of ideal Victorian
womanhood, it commands that some aspects of female
experience, especially anger and resentment, be
"avoided, denied, or suppressed." While Woolf
avoided them, some women writers drained their
energies trying to present these aspects in
"covert, risk-free ways." Today women are
beginning to deal more openly with their
experience.

312. _____ "Women Writers and the Female
      Experience." Notes from the Third Year:
      Women's Liberation (1971), 134-141.

      Argues that women writers have not escaped
the "hostile stereotypes and repressive practices
which have bound them from the beginning in their
literary undertakings." They have been prevented
from fully exploring and expressing their female
experiences by a double critical standard, a
double social standard, external censorship, and
self-censorship. Charlotte'Bronte's Jane Eyre,
George Eliot's Adam Bede, Kate Chopin's The
Awakening, and Mary McCarthy's The Group are
analyzed in support of the thesis.

313. Spencer, Sharon. "'Femininity' and the Woman
      Writer: Doris Lessing's The Golden Notebook
      and The Diary of Anais Nin." Women's Studies,
      1, No. 3 (1973), 247-257.

      Comments on the lack of female artist
characters in fiction by women. Women writers
have probably hesitated to fictionalize themselves
because of social prejudice against them. Self-
exposure would invite ridicule and rejection and
cause personal anxiety. Women writers have tended
to reveal themselves in less public genres such as
letters, diaries, and journals. Discusses Lessing
and Nin and their conflict between desire to
portray the woman artist and anxiety about their
"femininity."

314. Sukenick, Lynn. "On Women and Fiction." The
     Authority of Experience: Essays in Feminist
     Criticism. Edited by Arlyn Diamond and Lee R.
     Edwards. Amherst, Mass.: University of
     Massachusetts Press, 1977. Pp. 28-44.

        Difficult essay, which contends that women
     writers are afflicted with "a consciousness of
     gender." They recognize that gender has been an
     important factor in the appraisal of women's
     writing and has led to negative evaluation. In our
     culture femininity is associated with sensibility
     and emotion, whereas reason and detachment are
     essential to the act of writing. Women learn that
     they are "supposed to do best what they need not
     express," and thus "women's voicelessness" is
     reinforced.

315. Sullivan, Victoria, and Hatch, James.
     "Introduction." Plays by and about Women: An
     Anthology. Edited by Victoria Sullivan and
     James Hatch. New York: Random House, 1973.
     Pp. vii-xv.

        Introduction to collection of 8 twentieth-
     century plays by women. Analyzes the plays in
     terms of "the distance that women have travelled in
     their awareness of themselves" from the first play
     in 1913 to the last in 1969. Also discusses
     prejudice against female writers, noting that the
     modern woman playwright has had to "fight against
     strong cultural taboos."

316. Weller, Sheila. "To Be a Poet." Mademoiselle,
     70 (Dec. 1969), 126-127, 159-162.

        Discusses various problems faced by
     contemporary American women poets. Their vocation
     often conflicts with their role as wife and
     mother, and they are discriminated against by
     publishers and anthologists. However, the women
     write excellent poetry because they "push
     themselves to the limits of possibility."
     Describes the background and education of several
     poets, with emphasis on Anne Waldman, Nikki
     Giovanni, and Louise Glück.

317. West, Rebecca. "Woman as Artist and Thinker."
     Woman's Coming of Age: A Symposium. Edited

by Samuel D. Schmalhausen and V. F. Calverton.
New York: Horace Liveright, Inc., 1931.
Pp. 369-382.

Argues that woman could "equal the performance
of man as thinker and artist," if it were not for
the hindrance of environmental factors such as
lack of education, time spent child bearing and
rearing, and the constant abuse of women writers by
critics. Works by women are judged not by their
merits but according to their "conformity to the
codes of sexual behavior laid down for women by
society." West sees one difference in the writings
of men and women: men have a "disposition to
violence" and women do not.

318. Woolf, Virginia. "Professions for Women." The
Death of the Moth and Other Essays. New
York: Harcourt, Brace and Co., 1942.
Pp. 235-242. Also in Collected Essays.
Vol. 2. New York: Harcourt, Brace & World,
1967. Pp. 284-289.

Women have succeeded in the writing profession
before the other professions because of the
cheapness of writing paper. In order to succeed,
however, they have had to kill the "Angel in the
House," that inner voice which says they must
conceal their true opinions and pretend to be pure
and genteel models of femininity. Women writers
are still "impeded by the extreme conventionality
of the other sex." They may kill the Angel but
they still cannot tell the truth about their
passions, their "experiences as a body."

319. _____. A Room of One's Own. New York:
Harcourt, Brace & World, 1929. 118pp.

The famous essay, superb in both content and
style. Describes the social and economic factors
which have prevented women from writing, especially
the lack of money and a room of their own.
Discusses stylistic differences between male and
female writers, criticizes the expression of
resentment and anger in writing by women, and
introduces the theory that great writing must be
androgynous.

320. _____. "Women and Fiction." Forum, 81 (Mar.
1929), 179-183. Also in Granite and Rainbow:
Essays by Virginia Woolf. New York: Harcourt,

Brace and Co., 1958. Pp. 76-84. Also in
Collected Essays. Vol. 2. New York:
Harcourt, Brace & World, 1967. Pp. 141-148.

Extremely condensed form of A Room of One's
Own. Contains the main ideas but not the
development and examples.

See also: 21, 33, 46, 57, 61, 68, 95, 123, 125, 158,
172, 186, 197, 215, 221, 224, 225, 234, 235,
243, 253, 261, 265, 276, 407

VIII. PHALLIC CRITICISM

321. Alta. "Like It Is." <u>Small</u> <u>Press</u> <u>Review</u>, 3, No. 3
(1972), 1-6.

   Discussion of male prejudice against poetry
by women. Much of the best women's poetry being
written today is never published; male publishers
and editors will accept a woman's poem only if it's
"self-deprecatory," "passive," or "gory."

322. Banning, Margaret Culkin. "The Problem of
   Popularity." <u>Saturday</u> <u>Review</u> <u>of</u> <u>Literature</u>,
   May 2, 1936, pp. 3-4.

   Criticizes Katharine Gerould (see #58) for
being contemptuous of popular women writers and
their readers. Critics do not encourage the
writing of good fiction when they show disdain for
a large reading public and when they separate
writers and readers according to sex.

323. Bryan, Mary E. "How Should Women Write?" <u>South-</u>
   <u>land</u> <u>Writers</u>: <u>Biographical</u> <u>and</u> <u>Critical</u>
   <u>Sketches</u> <u>of</u> <u>the</u> <u>Living</u> <u>Female</u> <u>Writers</u> <u>of</u> <u>the</u>
   <u>South.</u> <u>With</u> <u>Extracts</u> <u>from</u> <u>Their</u> <u>Writings</u>.
   Edited by Ida Raymond [Mary T. Tardy].
   Vol. II. Philadelphia: Clexton, Remson &
   Haffelfinger, 1870. Pp. 664-668. Originally
   published in <u>Southern</u> <u>Field</u> <u>and</u> <u>Fireside</u>, 1
   (Jan. 1860).

   Protests the limitations imposed on women
writers. Men have not allowed women full freedom
to write. "They may flutter out of the cage, but
it must be with clipped wings." Male critics
severely limit the topics upon which women can
write without being attacked as "unfeminine," and
then they condemn her work as "tame and
commonplace." Women must be permitted to write
"honestly and without fear."

324. Cantarow, Ellen. "The Radicalizing of a Teacher of
     Literature." Change, 4 (May 1972), 50-61.
     Also in The Politics of Literature: Dissenting
     Essays on the Teaching of English as "Why
     Teach Literature? An Account of How I Came
     to Ask That Question." Edited by Louis Kampf
     and Paul Lauter. New York: Vintage Books,
     1973. (1st pub. 1972) Pp. 354-411.

     Critique of traditional literary criticism.
     The author recounts her experiences as student and
     teacher of literature, especially her gradual
     disenchantment with the masculinist "new criticism"
     and her realization in graduate school "that the
     gender of the critical mind . . . was masculine,
     and that to be a critic I would have to neuter my
     understanding."

325. Cotter, James Finn. "Women Poets: Malign
     Neglect?" America, Jan. 13, 1973, pp. 140-
     142.

     Argues that "women who are poets have much
     more trouble winning recognition than do men."
     In contemporary anthologies poems by women rarely
     comprise more than 10% of the selections. Male
     critics accept only those poets who, like
     Elizabeth Bishop and Marianne Moore, possess
     "intellectual coolness" and "metaphysical
     ingenuity"; in order to win critical recognition,
     women poets are forced to avoid female themes.

326. Edwards, Lee R., and Diamond, Arlyn.
     "Introduction." American Voices, American
     Women. Edited by Lee R. Edwards and Arlyn
     Diamond. New York: Avon, 1973. Pp. 11-18.

     Criticizes standard characterizations of the
     American literary tradition for ignoring works by
     women. In their preoccupation with themes of
     "Wilderness, Apocalypse, and Escape," critics have
     failed to consider the themes of women writers,
     especially their cry for "reconsideration of the
     nature of feminine identity."

327. Ellmann, Mary. Thinking about Women. New York:
     Harcourt Brace Jovanovich, Inc., 1968. 229pp.

     Witty dissection of sexual prejudices and
     stereotypes which pervade literary criticism.
     Discusses "sexual analogy," the use of the language

93

of sex to describe literary activity; "phallic"
criticism; feminine stereotypes; and the
differences between male and female writers.
Ellmann does not believe there is any specifically
feminine literary style but sees differences in
tone between women and men writers. She notes with
approval that women tend to rely less on the
"authoritative mode" of narration.

328. Gardener, H. H. "The Immoral Influence of Women
          in Literature." Arena, 1 (Feb. 1890),
          322-335.

          Attacks critics who complain of women's
      "immoral influence." First critics considered it
      immodest for women to write at all; now they
      encourage women to "reflect ready-made masculine
      opinions." As a result, the female character in
      fiction is still "what men fancy she is or ought to
      be." Women should be allowed to write as they
      please.

329. Gardiner, Dorothy. "The Woman Writer and the
          Paperback Market." Publisher's Weekly,
          Apr. 21, 1956, pp. 1784-1786.

          Claims that the woman mystery writer "is
      being squeezed out of the hardcover field and is
      rejected by the paperbacks." Publishers believe
      that the "quiet" mysteries, which women most often
      write, do not sell in the paperback market. Quotes
      one publisher as saying, "There is today a definite
      prejudice in the paperback field against any book
      written by a woman, mystery or otherwise."

330. Goulianos, Joan. "Introduction." By a Woman
          Writt: Literature from Six Centuries by and
          about Women. Edited by Joan Goulianos.
          Baltimore: Penguin Books, 1974. (1st pub.
          1973) Pp. xiii-xix.

          Considers the question of what the writers
      represented in the anthology have in common.
      They described women's experiences, used similar
      literary forms, and wrote in a world controlled by
      men. "It was men who were the critics, the
      publishers, the professors, the sources of support,
      It was men who had the power to praise women's
      works, to bring them to public attention, or to
      ridicule them, to doom them--as was done to many of
      the works in this book--to obscurity."

331. Higginson, Thomas Wentworth. "The Lilliputian
       Theory of Woman." Concerning All of Us. New
       York: Harper and Brothers, 1892. Pp. 22-29.

       Deplores the tendency of critics, especially
       female critics, to belittle women. Those who try
       to deny that women possess creative genius usually
       ignore the great women writers and set up a test
       of immortality which most women cannot pass because
       they have not been writing long enough. Obviously
       a response to Seawell (#266), though does not
       mention her by name.

332. "Lady Novelists." Living Age, 357 (Oct. 1939),
       188-190.

       Quotes extensively from Cyril Joad's
       misogynist essay in New Statesman & Nation and
       Naomi Mitchison's letter rebuking him (see #241).
       The critical controversy is unfortunate, as "one
       feels an undercurrent of malice on one side and
       resentment on the other."

333. Lathrop, George Parsons. "Audacity in Women
       Novelists." North American Review, 150
       (May 1890), 609-617. Discussion, 151 (July
       1890), 127-128.

       Anticipates modern discussions of androgynous
       art. Argues that the mind of the great writer must
       be "free, observant, and independent" and must
       "unite some of the elements of both sexes." When
       male critics try to limit the province of female
       novelists, they are severely damaging women's
       capacity as authors. Women must be allowed to
       express themselves freely, even to the point of
       dealing with "sin and vice and crime."

       Discussion - Attacks the article, claiming that
       even the word "audacity" is "repulsive to the
       instinctive delicacy of every true woman."

334. Mackey, Mary. "Women's Poetry: Almost Subversive."
       Small Press Review, 3, No. 3 (1972), 17.

       Contends that women have difficulty
       publishing their poetry because the male critics,
       editors, and publishers prefer poetry which is
       "obscure, symbolic, magical, abstract,
       inaccessible"; the poem must make the poet seem
       superior to the reader, must, in fact, be a grab

for power. Female poets speak clearly and are
less egotistic.

335. Morgan, Robin. "Conspiracy of Silence against a
          Feminist Poem." Feminist Art Journal, 1
          (Fall 1972), 4-5, 21.

       Detailed account of Morgan's attempts to
publish her poem "Arraignment," which accuses Ted
Hughes of Sylvia Plath's murder; neither Random
House nor Ms. would print the original version,
which appears here. Article includes general
discussion of the publishing world and feminist
writers' difficulty in reaching a wide audience.

336. Ozick, Cynthia. "We Are the Crazy Lady and Other
          Feisty Feminist Fables." Ms., 1 (Spring
          1972), 40-44.

       Author's personal experience as a victim of
sex prejudice. Includes an interesting account of
the writing of her first published novel. She
labored to make her female narrator a mechanical
device, rather than a real character, because she
was "afraid to be pegged as having written a
'woman's' novel." Reviewers then emphasized the
"feminine sensibility" of her narrator.

337. Repplier, Agnes. "The Literary Lady." Atlantic
          Monthly, 101 (Feb. 1908), 263-269.

       Through pretended nostalgia for the good old
days when women writers were "praised and petted,"
the author attacks male critics. Early British
"literary ladies," whose accomplishments were few,
were indulged by critics. But the men turned on
female authors when "they stepped . . . from their
appointed spheres and hotly challenged the
competition of the world."

338. _____. "The Point of View." Compromises.
          Boston: Houghton, Mifflin and Co., 1904.
          Pp. 34-48.

       Notes that male critics have consistently
complained about the male heroes in novels by
women. If this means that "femininity, backed by
genius, cannot grasp the impalpable something which
is the soul and essence of masculinity," then "it
follows that masculinity, backed by genius, cannot

grasp the impalpable something which is the soul
and essence of femininity. Such a limitation has
never yet been recognized and deplored" by critics.

339. Rexroth, Kenneth. "Introduction." Four Young
     Women Poets. Edited by Kenneth Rexroth.
     New York: McGraw-Hill Book Co., 1973.
     Pp. ix-xi.

     Brief introduction to the work of 4 young
poets. Claims that "the majority of students who
write poetry are women and usually they write
better than the men." However, after age 25 they
begin to disappear--"they find it very hard indeed
to get published."

340. Showalter, Elaine. "Women Writers and the Double
     Standard." Woman in Sexist Society: Studies
     in Power and Powerlessness. Edited by Vivian
     Gornick and Barbara K. Moran. New York:
     Basic Books, Inc., 1971. Pp. 452-479.

     Shows how nineteenth-century women writers
were "measured against a feminine, rather than a
literary, ideal" and how they resented this unequal
treatment. Critics held a double standard of
literary abilities which heavily favored men.
Men's writing was considered to possess the most
desireable traits--"power, breadth, distinctness,
clarity, learning, understanding of history and
abstraction, shrewdness, knowledge of life, and
humor." Women's work was considered deficient in
these qualities but superior in refinement and
domestic detail. Examples are from English
critics.

341. Stasio, Marilyn. "The Nights the Critics Lost
     Their Cool." Ms., 4 (Sept. 1975), 37-41.

     Suggests that "the male-heavy critical
community, with its male-oriented reactions" is
responsible for the small number of women now
writing for the commercial theater. Little of the
experimental drama being written by women makes its
way into mainstream theater, and when it does the
critics' response is frequently "obtuse,
insensitive, and unencouraging." More female drama
critics are needed.

See also: 23, 28, 32, 87, 108, 127, 234, 243, 282, 285,
           291, 292, 293, 299, 305, 312, 314, 317, 318

97

IX. FEMINIST LITERARY CRITICISM

342.   Barnes, Annette. "Female Criticism: A Prologue."
       The Authority of Experience: Essays in
       Feminist Criticism. Edited by Arlyn Diamond
       and Lee R. Edwards. Amherst, Mass.:
       University of Massachusetts Press, 1977.
       Pp. 1-15.

           Abstract discussion of whether it is possible
       for critics to be objective. Attempts to define
       "feminist perspective" and gives examples from
       recent criticism designed to show that "female
       critics (in particular feminists) are neither more
       nor less partisan than their male counterparts."

343.   Broyard, Anatole. "Women as Stud: An Inquiry into
       Fem. Lit." Mademoiselle, 79 (July 1974),
       98-99, 117-118.

           Tirade against feminist novelists and critics.
       Makes extended analogy between women's books and
       their sex organs, concluding that "the reviewing
       of feminist novels has come to resemble the
       gynecological self-help clinic." Heroines of many
       feminist novels are "female studs," and women
       critics do nothing but applaud. Broyard resents
       "the closed circle approach to women's writing"--
       what he sees as feminist women's unwillingness to
       be reviewed by men. It is unfair to say that men
       cannot understand women; after all, "Who is
       closer to a woman than an American boy to his
       mother?"

344.   Diamond, Arlyn, and Edwards, Lee R. "Foreword."
       The Authority of Experience: Essays in
       Feminist Criticism. Edited by Arlyn Diamond
       and Lee R. Edwards. Amherst, Mass.:
       University of Massachusetts Press, 1977.
       Pp. ix-xiv.

           States that feminist literary criticism is not
       a "school of criticism with a rigidly defined

methodology." However, feminist critics do share
many assumptions about literature and criticism.
They approach literature in terms of its wider
social contexts and attempt to "measure literary
reality on the one side against historical and
personally felt reality on the other."

345.   Donovan, Josephine. "Afterword: Critical
       Re-Vision." Feminist Literary Criticism:·
       Explorations in Theory. Edited by Josephine
       Donovan. Lexington, Ky.: University Press of
       Kentucky, 1975. Pp. 74-81.

       Describes feminist criticism as a dialectical
process. It is a "mode of negation" in that
feminist critics are negating the reification of
patriarchal attitudes in literature and literary
criticism; but, on the other hand, feminist critics
are creating new paradigms, such as the concepts of
androgyny and female culture, and are moving
"toward and into transcending consciousness."

346.   _____, ed. Feminist Literary Criticism:
       Explorations in Theory. Lexington, Ky.:
       University Press of Kentucky, 1975. 81pp.

       Collection of six essays, intended to "present
an interpretation, and in some sense a defense, of
feminist literary criticism." According to the
editor, the essays are "ordered for the reader who
knows little about feminist criticism"; however,
they do demand a reader schooled in the language
and methods of literary criticism.

347.   Efros, Susan. "Introduction." This Is Women's
       Work: An Anthology of Prose and Poetry.
       Edited by Susan Efros. San Francisco:
       Panjandrum Press, 1974. Pp. ix-xi.

       Introduction to anthology of poems and short
stories by young American women. Emphasis is on
the necessity for using "stringent criteria" in
publishing and criticizing works by women. Women
should be supportive of each other's work, but
"supportiveness must be coupled with honesty and
strict, professional criticism."

348.   Gornick, Vivian. "Feminist Writers: Hanging
            Ourselves on a Party Line?" Ms., 4 (July
            1975), 104-107.

        Deplores the effect of "party opinion" in the
Women's Movement on feminist literary criticism.
Much critical observation stems from a political
rather than intellectual position. If a work by
a woman is "woman-identified," it is praised;
otherwise it is condemned. If a review of a
woman's work is by a man, the review is a priori
bad; if the review is by a woman and is at all
unfavorable, it is considered traitorous. This
kind of criticism is ultimately harmful to women.

349.   Heilbrun, Carolyn, and Stimpson, Catharine.
            "Theories of Feminist Criticism: A Dialogue."
            Feminist Literary Criticism: Explorations in
            Theory. Edited by Josephine Donovan.
            Lexington, Ky.: University Press of Kentucky,
            1975. Pp. 61-73.

        Attempt to distinguish two approaches to
feminist criticism through a debate between two
critics, "X" and "Y." The dialogue is very
abstract, and it is not always easy to see the
differences in approach. In general, Y is more
socially conscious than X and less accepting of
formalist criticism; she relates the literary
patterns she finds to social and political
structures and hopes for social action. X stresses
the individual imagination and advocates textual
analysis as a way of revealing "new meanings about
human possibilities"; she hopes to involve men in
the "female experience."

350.   Hoffman, Nancy; Secor, Cynthia; and Tinsley,
            Adrian. "Feminist Criticism: Introduction."
            Female Studies VI: Closer to the Ground:
            Women's Classes, Criticism, Programs-1972.
            Edited by Nancy Hoffman, Cynthia Secor, and
            Adrian Tinsley. Old Westbury, N. Y.: Feminist
            Press, 1972. Pp. 99-101.

        Describes several functions of feminist
criticism. One function is to examine the
representation of women in literature; a second,
more challenging function is to raise the question
"Need women and men have distinctly different
consciousnesses?" In general, feminist critics
must reveal the masculine bias in literature and

"develop a theory of literary history, of literary genre, and of literary technique that does justice to the feminine consciousness and feminine culture."

351. Hoffman, Nancy Jo. "Reading Women's Poetry: The Meaning and Our Lives." College English, 34 (Oct. 1972), 48-62.

Argues that women's poetry portrays woman as "victim of her powerlessness, not as actor in the process of change." The two predominant types of feminist criticism--describing feminine stereotypes and analyzing motifs in women's literature--do not provide readers with a model for change. A third type is needed, one which constructs "a vision of the future, a model of the positive process of change. . . . If this process does not exist in literature by women, it can come alive in a community of women readers who define criticism as a mediation between poetry and their own lives."

352. Holly, Marcia. "Consciousness and Authenticity: Toward a Feminist Aesthetic." Feminist Literary Criticism: Explorations in Theory. Edited by Josephine Donovan. Lexington, Ky.: University Press of Kentucky, 1975. Pp. 38-47.

Argues that feminist criticism is a step in the development of "a feminist literary aesthetic--one that is fundamentally at odds with masculinist value standards, measuring literature against an understanding of authentic female life." In order to recognize authenticity, or its lack, in a literary work, critics must be aware of sexual stereotyping and bring to a conscious level their own beliefs about the nature of women.

353. Howe, Florence. "Feminism, Fiction, and the Classroom." Soundings, 55 (Winter 1972), 369-389. Also in Images of Women in Fiction: Feminist Perspectives. Edited by Susan Koppelman Cornillon. Bowling Green, Ohio: Bowling Green University Popular Press, 1972. Pp. 253-277.

Nicely written essay, combining the public and the personal, on the connections between feminism and literature and between women's lives and their

work. Traces the "discontinuity" between her own
life and work before the feminist movement, then
her recognition that supposedly "universal" writers
like Joyce and Lawrence actually have a limited
masculine vision. Ends with her discovery of
"lost" women writers, such as Kate Chopin and
Tillie Olsen.

354. Howe, Florence. "A Report on Women and the
Profession." College English, 32 (May 1971),
847-854.

Paper read as introduction to the Modern
Language Association Forum on Women in the
Profession, Dec. 27, 1970. Reviews the status of
female academics in the language and literature
field and comments on literary criticism. Critics
and teachers have "helped to misshape our
perceptions about the nature and roles of women"
and have created a male-dominated curriculum and a
male-centered criticism. Feminists must work to
correct this situation.

355. Iverson, Lucille. "Preface." We Become New:
Poems by Contemporary Women. Edited by
Lucille Iverson and Kathryn Ruby. New York:
Bantam Books, 1975. Pp. xviii-xxi.

Attempts to define feminist poetry as
distinct from women's poetry. Feminist poetry
"springs from and speaks about the intimate and
personal lives of women." It projects an image of
the self-defined woman and is clear, revolutionary,
and often angry.

356. Kaplan, Ann. "Feminist Criticism: A Survey with
Analysis of Methodological Problems."
University of Michigan Papers in Women's
Studies, 1 (Feb. 1974), 150-177.

Criticizes pre-1970 books on women writers for
striving to be "objective" and thus achieving no
perspective. New feminist critics have taken three
main approaches: focus on portrayal of women by men
writers, analysis of literature from a Marxist-
feminist standpoint, and research into forgotten
works by women. Kaplan sees the latter approach
as most fruitful; the first two are limited because
the perspective does not arise out of literary or
aesthetic concerns. "High art" must be seen
"within a larger context than sexism." Essay is

thought-provoking but full of contradictions, and
it is finally unclear from what "perspective" or
"larger context" literary works can be viewed.

357. Katz-Stoker, Fraya. "The Other Criticism:
          Feminism vs. Formalism." Images of Women in
          Fiction: Feminist Perspectives. Edited by
          Susan Koppelman Cornillon. Bowling Green,
          Ohio: Bowling Green University Popular Press,
          1972. Pp. 315-327.

          Sees feminist criticism as a healthy challenge
and alternative to formalist criticism, which is
alienated and helps preserve the status quo.
"Feminist criticism is a materialist approach to
literature which attempts to do away with the
formalist illusion that literature is somehow
divorced from the rest of reality."

358. Kolodny, Annette. "The Feminist as Literary
          Critic." Critical Inquiry, 2 (Summer 1976),
          821-832.

          Reply to William W. Morgan's criticism (#366)
of her essay (#360). In speaking of the need to
separate political ideologies from aesthetic
judgments, she meant only that feminist critics
must avoid being doctrinaire and "imprisoned by
ideology." As for Morgan's objection to feminist
criticism being a separate branch of criticism
practiced by women, the separation Morgan should be
concerned with is the "separation of men from the
dominant control of power in academia." Only this
would signal the "revolution" of which Morgan
speaks.

359. _____. "Review Essay: Literary Criticism."
          Signs, 2 (Winter 1976), 404-421.

          Survey of feminist criticism in 1975. Finds
the year's work disappointing, revealing a
"critical stasis." The "cataloging of stereotypic
images of women" is still dominant, while many
female novelists and poets are ignored. Feminist
criticism is unevenly practiced, being "more like
a set of interchangeable strategies than any
coherent school or shared goal orientation."

360. Kolodny, Annette. "Some Notes on Defining a
     'Feminist Literary Criticism.'" Critical
     Inquiry, 2 (Aug. 1975), 75-92.

     Contends that no one has yet defined feminist
     criticism or demonstrated what is unique about
     women's literary expression. Feminist critics
     should stop assuming that women write differently
     from men and start considering how to discover
     whether or not they do. It is necessary to
     "separate political ideologies from aesthetic
     judgments" and treat each author as an individual,
     finally checking to see if certain themes, images,
     and stylistic traits recur in women's writings.
     For a time feminist criticism must be by and for
     women because only women have the experience
     necessary to understand and evaluate female
     authors.

361. Lamb, Margaret. "Feminist Criticism." Drama
     Review, 18 (Sept. 1974), 46-50.

     Complains that plays by women are not
     well-covered, even in the feminist press.
     Feminist drama criticism is needed in several
     areas: women in theater history, women in
     contemporary theater, and "criticism of critics,
     particularly of what they leave out."

362. Landy, Marcia. "The Silent Woman: Towards a
     Feminist Critique." The Authority of
     Experience: Essays in Feminist Criticism.
     Edited by Arlyn Diamond and Lee R. Edwards.
     Amherst, Mass.: University of Massachusetts
     Press, 1977. Pp. 16-27.

     Abstruse essay on various "dimensions"
     involved in a "feminist critique." Three of the
     dimensions are "examination of the mythology
     embedded in the art of the past," exploration of
     "whether fictional language and structure must
     reflect the sex of the creator," and study of
     "signification." States that the female writer
     suffers "from the problem of conversion to
     language out of her traditional silence, and from
     the problem which most writers face of
     experiencing language as silence."

363. Lebowitz, Andrea. "Some Recent Feminist
         Criticism." West Coast Review, 10 (Feb.
         1976), 61-63.

         Review of recent feminist literary criticism.
      Argues that "exposing the political, social and
      literary exploitation of women in literature" is
      a less interesting and useful aspect of feminist
      criticism than analyzing "the particular
      imagination and technique of women writers."

364. McDowell, Margaret B. "Reflections on the New
         Feminism." Midwest Quarterly, 12 (Apr. 1971),
         309-333.

         Wide-ranging review of Kate Millett's Sexual
      Politics. Discusses several feminist critics and
      addresses the question of how literary criticism
      should be handled in works on the position of
      women. Millett's literary criticism is seen as
      "reductive" and "one-sided"; she presents fictional
      passages out of context and equates the attitudes
      of characters and authors. Also, analysis of
      fiction by women would be "more pertinent to an
      understanding of woman's position" than analysis
      of fiction by men. The main problem facing
      feminist critics is "the difficulty of reconciling
      scholarship and perceptive literary criticism with
      effective political action."

365. Martin, Wendy, and Briscoe, Mary Louise. "Women's
         Studies: Problems in Research." Women's
         Studies, 2, No. 2 (1974), 249-259.

         Two essays on trends in feminist criticism.
      Both writers find the most activity in the study of
      sexism in literature. Martin believes it is time
      to pay more attention to neglected and emerging
      women writers. Briscoe emphasizes the need for a
      variety of approaches and calls for more
      bibliographic work.

366. Morgan, William W. "Feminism and Literary Study:
         A Reply to Annette Kolodny." Critical
         Inquiry, 2 (Summer 1976), 807-816.

         Criticizes Kolodny's essay (#360) for
      advocating two damaging kinds of separatism.
      Political ideologies cannot be separated from
      aesthetic judgments because the two are
      necessarily intertwined. Moreover, feminist

criticism should not remain a separate criticism restricted to women because, if it has "revolutionary implications for literary study," it is everyone's concern.

367. Pratt, Annis. "Archetypal Approaches to the New Feminist Criticism." Bucknell Review, 21 (Spring 1973), 3-14.

Argues that, although Jung, Frye, and Campbell assume the human soul is male, some of their insights can be used by feminist critics in the "elucidation of the psycho-mythological development of the female hero." Answers Robinson's criticism (#375) of her 1971 article, saying we must have analysis of the "internal-psychic components" in women's experience, as well as the external-material.

368. _____. "The New Feminist Criticism." College English, 32 (May 1971), 872-878.

Identifies four critical modes which can be adapted for feminist criticism: bibliographic, textual, contextual, and archetypal. The bibliographic mode involves identification of feminist works and the textual mode judgment of the formal aspects of particular texts. Contextual analysis considers "the relevance of a group of works, even if artistically flawed, as a reflection of the situation of women." The archetypal mode of criticism can be used to describe the "psycho-mythological development of the female individual in literature."

369. _____. "The New Feminist Criticisms: Exploring the History of the New Space." Beyond Intellectual Sexism: A New Woman, A New Reality. Edited by Joan I. Roberts. New York: David McKay Co., Inc., 1976. Pp. 175-195.

Asserts that "there is room in the new feminist criticisms for a variety of methodologies" and lists several types, with examples of each. Presents some tentative conclusions from her application of "textual, contextual, and archetypal" modes of criticism to women's novels of the past 200 years. Appended to the article is an outline of patterns in this fiction and suggestions for further research.

370. Register, Cheri. "American Feminist Literary
        Criticism: A Bibliographical Introduction."
        Feminist Literary Criticism: Explorations in
        Theory. Edited by Josephine Donovan.
        Lexington, Ky.: University Press of Kentucky,
        1975. Pp. 1-28.

        Bibliographic essay which attempts to define
        feminist criticism and illustrate its functions.
        Feminist criticism is divided into three
        categories: 1) examination of images of women in
        literary works by men; 2) analysis of existing
        criticism of female authors; and 3) "prescriptive"
        criticism. The third type, which is the newest
        and least clearly formulated, "attempts to set
        standards for literature that is 'good' from a
        feminist viewpoint." It may become "the crux of
        feminist criticism in the future."

371. _____. "'But You Couldn't Possibly Be Objective
        about . . .': Feminism and Graduate Research."
        Female Studies VIII. Edited by Sarah Slavin
        Schramm. National Organization for Women,
        [1974]. Pp. 204-209.

        Discussion of objectivity and feminist
        criticism. Recounts her difficulties defining her
        critical method in her dissertation and considers
        various types and functions of feminist criticism.

372. Reuben, Elaine. "Can a Young Girl from a Small
        Mining Town Find Happiness Writing Criticism
        for The New York Review of Books?" College
        English, 34 (Oct. 1972), 39-47.

        The answer is no. There is little likelihood
        that she will get an assignment, for the essence of
        the critical role is authority, and "woman" and
        "authority" are "virtually antonymic in our
        culture." If the Young Girl does become a critic,
        she will be pressured to isolate herself from other
        women and pose as a "superior" woman. Doing this
        requires a lack of sympathy towards and
        understanding of other women and "a resulting lack
        of critical, moral clarity." Elizabeth Hardwick
        and Mary McCarthy are discussed as examples.

373. Reuben, Elaine. "Feminist Criticism in the
     Classroom, or, 'What Do You Mean We, White
     Man?'" Women's Studies, 1, No. 3 (1973),
     315-325.

     Claims the task of feminist criticism in the
     classroom is "to analyze the class nature of a
     predominantly white male literary tradition." It
     is not enough, however, to point out sexism in
     literary works; the teacher and students must
     explore the social and personal implications of
     their analyses.

374. Richmond, Velma Bourgeois. "Women as Critics:
     A Look to the Future." CEA Critic, 37
     (May 1975), 20-22.

     Takes feminist critics to task for what she
     sees as "negativistic attack and hostile
     rebellion." Too much time is spent documenting
     abuses, and the "search for anti-feminism" leads
     to distortion and misreading. The weakness of
     feminist criticism is "the polemical nature of the
     writing, and its very limited interest." In the
     future female critics should be "more diversified
     and discriminating" and emphasize hard work and
     discretion.

375. Robinson, Lillian S. "Dwelling in Decencies:
     Radical Criticism and the Feminist
     Perspective." College English, 32 (May 1971),
     879-889.

     Discussion of feminist criticism from a
     Marxist point of view. Fears feminist criticism
     will become bourgeois and be used, like
     traditional criticism, "in the service of ruling-
     class interests." Criticizes Pratt's four modes
     for feminist criticism (#368) as "firmly
     entrenched in standard lit-crit assumptions";
     textual criteria are falsely seen as being
     independent of ideology. Theré is no "objective"
     or "disinterested" criticism, and feminist
     criticism "must be ideological and moral criticism;
     it must be revolutionary."

376. Sagan, Miriam. "Feminist Literary Criticism."
      Feminist Art Journal, 5 (Winter 1976-77),
      38-40.

      Review of Donovan (#346), Moers (#132) and
      Spacks (#270). Defines feminist literary criticism
      as "an examination of the common areas of concern
      which women writers share because of their
      sex-determined experience." The future tasks of
      feminist critics are further definition of the
      presence of female subculture and imagination in
      literature and exploration of new ways of dealing
      with literature by women.

377. Schumacher, Dorin. "Subjectivities: A Theory of
      the Critical Process." _Feminist Literary
      Criticism_: Explorations in Theory. Edited by
      Josephine Donovan. Lexington, Ky.:
      University Press of Kentucky, 1975.
      Pp. 29-37.

      Discusses the nature of the critical process
      and concludes that feminist criticism is not a new
      type of criticism with different methods but
      "simply a new form of sex-linked criticism."
      Feminist criticism has reversed the assumptions of
      masculinist criticism, taking woman as "self," or
      normative, and man as "other," or deviant.

378. Showalter, Elaine. "Review Essay: Literary
      Criticism." _Signs_, 1 (Winter 1975), 435-460.
      Discussion, 1 (Spring 1976), 771-772.

      Review of the "most useful work" done in
      feminist criticism in the past five years.
      Feminist criticism has gone beyond analysis of
      sexism in male novels, to the resurrection of
      "lost" women writers and the reinterpretation of
      well-known women writers. It has made use of
      methodologies from Marxist and structural
      criticism and of materials from linguistics,
      psychology, anthropology, art history, and social
      history. But so far feminist critics have been
      empirical and have created no "solid system of
      critical theory."

      Discussion - Marjorie G. Perloff disagrees with
      Showalter's comment that women writers should
      struggle against verbal inhibition and forge a
      language of the body. Female writers have been too
      busy "fighting men on their turf," rather than
      evaluating their own experiences as women.

379. Showalter, Elaine. "Women and the Literary
     Curriculum." College English, 32 (May 1971),
     855-862.

        Criticizes the traditional literary curriculum
     in the university for ignoring women writers,
     except as an object of scorn. Provides a rationale
     for treating women writers as a group in literary
     criticism or literature classes. "Women writers
     should not be studied as a distinct group on the
     assumption that they write alike, or even display
     stylistic resemblances distinctively feminine.
     But women do have a special literary history
     susceptible to analysis."

380. Women's Studies. Vol. 2, No. 2 (1974).

        Papers from the December 1973 Modern Language
     Association Forum, "Androgyny: Fact or Fiction."
     Most are relevant to feminist criticism because
     they deal with the concept of androgyny, and
     whether feminists should see it as an ideal to be
     emulated or a reactionary tool to be rejected.

381. Yeazell, Ruth. "Fictional Heroines and Feminist
     Critics." Novel, 8 (Fall 1974), 29-38.

        Attack on feminist literary criticism, with
     very few examples from the criticism provided.
     Feminist critics "run the risk of sacrificing
     literature to polemic, of seeing red so quickly
     that they are blinded to the subtler shades and
     tones." Feminist critics often refuse to read
     metaphorically, treating novels as literal
     transcriptions of life, and their "stereotype-
     hunting" leads them to impose patterns on the
     literature which do not exist.

See also: 31, 62, 98, 101, 227, 270, 311, 319, 320, 324

X. MISCELLANEOUS

382. Abbot, A. W. "Female Authors." North American
Review, 72 (Jan. 1851), 151-177.

Review essay which contends that women writers
are wounded by unfavorable criticism and expect
"indulgent sympathy" from readers and critics.
Women deserve such sympathy so long as they produce
"graceful little tales" describing nature or
embodying moral and religious truths; however,
they must not forget the privileges extended to
them and agitate for women's rights.

383. Abernethy, J. W. "The Womanliness of Literary
Women." Lippincott's, 55 (Apr. 1895),
570-576.

Chides women writers for lacking restraint
and writing too much that is strident and shocking.
Women now have full equality with men, but this
shouldn't mean "immunity from the elemental
responsibilities inherent in the fact of womanhood." Female authors must bring to literature
"the beauty, delicacy, ideality, and grace of
femininity." George Eliot was a great novelist,
but she also remained "womanly" in her writing.

384. Bitker, Marjorie M. "Time for Sale." Writer,
75 (Feb. 1962), 14-16.

Bits of advice for women on how to make time
to write and how to deal with publishers.

385. Boyd, Ernest A. "Portrait of a Literary Lady."
Bookman, 59 (Apr. 1924), 195-200. Also in
Portraits: Real and Imaginary as "A Literary
Lady." New York: George H. Doran Co., 1924.
Pp. 26-35.

Satirical account of a "literary lady" on her
way to fame. Portrays her as a midwestern villager

sending love poems to a male editor, moving East,
having an affair with another editor, etc. The
point of the satire is that the "literary lady"
relies on femininity and charm to get ahead but
underneath is hard, ambitious, and even ruthless.

386. Brotherton, Alice Williams. "The Husbands of
Literary Women." Writer, 3 (Dec. 1889),
269-270.

Claims that the husbands of literary women are
no longer ridiculed but are envied. The woman
writer looks to her husband for "sympathy,
criticism and practical advice"; he is usually the
"mainspring of her activity."

387. College English, 32 (May 1971).

"Women in the Colleges" issue. Contains
essays on the status of female professors, teaching
women's studies, and feminist criticism. Many of
the articles were written at the request of the
Modern Language Association (MLA) Commission on
Women and read at the Forum on Women in the
Profession during the 1970 annual MLA meeting.

388. College English, 34 (Oct. 1972).

Special issue on "Women Writing and Teaching."
Contains several papers from the Forum on the Woman
Writer in the Twentieth Century held at the Modern
Language Association Convention in 1971.

389. Convocation! Women in Writing. Edited by Valerie
Harms. Tampa, Fla.: United Sisters, 1975.
178pp.

Account of the Writers Conference sponsored
by NOW in 1974. Besides descriptions of speeches,
panels and workshops, includes Sharon Spencer's
"Manifesto of a Woman Writer" and Megan Terry's
comments on female playwrights.

390. Deland, Margaret. "The Girl Who Writes." Harper's
Bazar, July 14, 1900, pp. 670-672.

Advises young women not to try to publish
their writings too quickly. They should widen
their experience of life and learn judgment.

391. Duer, Caroline. "Ideals of American Womanhood:
The Literary Woman." Harper's Weekly, May 23,
1903, p. 833.

Advises women to be "patient and painstaking"
with their writing. Claims that women are
"inclined to force their talents when they have
once resolved to use them, and the result is not
always permanently successful."

392. Evans, Nancy Burr. "The Value and Peril for Women
of Reading Women Writers." Images of Women in
Fiction: Feminist Perspectives. Edited by
Susan Koppelman Cornillon. Bowling Green,
Ohio: Bowling Green University Popular Press,
1972. Pp. 308-314.

The value is self-understanding and impetus
toward social change. The peril is over-
identification and a possible "dead-end response."
"An identification through mutual oppression as
women which should initially lead to an awakening
and then to action can quite conveniently be
manipulated to become a comfort, an excuse not
only for societal ills but personal ones as well."

393. "Feminine Fiction." Saturday Review, Dec. 1, 1894,
p. 556.

Claims that women writers are clever but not
great; they lack the motives of the "true artist"
and want only to be envied and admired.
"Feminine fiction . . . lives before the mirror; it
is like a beautiful, low-necked evening dress, worn
in order that the wearer may be admired by men and
envied by women."

394. Fern, Fanny. [Sara Willis Parton.] "A Chapter
on Literary Women." Fern Leaves from Fanny's
Port-folio. Auburn, N. Y.: Derby and Miller,
1853. Pp. 175-179.

Discussion by popular nineteenth-century
American novelist of the merits of "literary
women." Takes the form of a dialogue between a man
and a woman, the man arguing that women who write
are ambitious and "unfeminine." The woman says
women write because "they can't help it"; they
have an unquenchable "heaven-kindled spark."
The conclusion is that "a woman may be literary,

113

and yet feminine and lovable; content to find her
greatest happiness in the charmed circle of Home."

395. Fern, Fanny. [Sara Willis Parton.] Folly as It
      Flies. New York: Carleton, 1870. (1st pub.
      1868) Pp. 61-64.

      Advocates writing as an outlet for women who
are frustrated and unhappy in their lives. Writing
can serve as an antidote to the fact that woman,
"once wound up by the marriage ceremony, is
expected to click on with undeviating monotony till
Death stops the hands."

396. Freeman, Mary E. Wilkins. "The Girl Who Wants to
      Write: Things to Do and to Avoid." Harper's
      Bazar, 47 (June 1913), 272.

      Advises prospective writers to put their work
before everything except duty to others. Since it
is important for America to have a distinctly
national literature, the writer should also make
her work "essentially of her own country."

397. Gilder, Jeannette L   "Does It Pay to Be a Literary
      Woman?" Leslie's Monthly Magazine, 60
      (May 1905), 3-12.

      Several women writers give an opinion on
whether young girls who aspire to a writing career
should be encouraged. Most speak favorably of the
literary life.

398. Greenwood, Grace. [Sara J. C. Lippincott.]
      "Letter I." Greenwood Leaves. 4th ed.
      Boston: Ticknor, Reed, and Fields, 1853.
      (1st ed. 1849) Pp. 309-313.

      Popular nineteenth-century American writer
warns women not to "unsex" themselves trying to
achieve literary greatness. Ambition is
unfeminine; the literary woman should put social
and domestic ties first. "True feminine genius is
ever timid, doubtful, and clingingly dependent;
a perpetual childhood."

399. Helson, Ravenna. "Inner Reality of Women." Arts
in Society, 11 (Spring-Summer 1974), 25-36.

Discussion of women artists, with emphasis on
writers. Sets forth results of a study she did on
female authors of fantasy for children since 1930.
Four types of creative personality emerged:
"adoption of outer reality," "concentration on
inner reality," "conflict between inner and outer
realities," and "mustering of inner reality and
defiance of society." The first type adopts the
feminine role in order to achieve success and
bestsellerdom, the second is attuned to nature
and inner life, the third criticizes society but
is self-blaming, and the last is able to avoid
traditional sex roles. The categories are not
very clearly presented, nor is their significance.

400. Howe, Florence. "Identity and Expression: A
Writing Course for Women." College English,
32 (May 1971), 863-871.

Describes her experiences teaching women to
write. Her women students have consistently
considered female writers inferior to male writers.
It is thus necessary to begin breaking their
"passive-dependent patterns and assumptions of
inferiority" and "informing them about the
processes of social conditioning, helping them to
analyze sexual stereotyping and to grow conscious
of themselves as women."

401. Images of Women in Fiction: Feminist Perspectives.
Edited by Susan Koppelman Cornillon. Bowling
Green, Ohio: Bowling Green University Popular
Press, 1972. 400pp.

Important collection of feminist essays on
women and literature. The first two sections
consist of analyses of conventional heroines. The
third section contains essays on fiction in which
women are portrayed as whole people and the fourth
section essays on feminist aesthetics. Contains
the first edition of the Sense & Sensibility
Collective's bibliography on women in literature.

402. Kirkland, Winifred. "The Woman Who Writes."
     Atlantic, 118 (July 1916), 46-54. Also in
     The Joys of Being a Woman and Other Papers.
     Cambridge, Mass.: Riverside Press, 1918.
     Pp. 129-153.

     Purports to be "an examination into the
     psychology and methods of the woman writer" by a
     free-lance writer. Actually a useful collection of
     the contemporary cliches and contradictory thinking
     on women writers. There have never been "any
     restrictions, commercial or social, to bar a
     woman's way to the literary career." Female
     writers are hampered by their inferior physique and
     intellect, but their intuition helps them in
     writing. However, "a real woman chooses living
     rather than literature," for a baby is more
     important than a book. The author herself writes
     only because she cannot help it--something compels
     her to write.

403. McCall, Anne Bryan. "The Girl Who Wants to Write."
     Woman's Home Companion, 37 (Oct. 1910), 24.

     Advice for aspiring writers; emphasizes the
     need for courage and patience.

404. Meade, Julian R. "Springtime Pilgrimage to the
     Gardens of Nine Women Who Wield a Spade as
     Well as a Pen." Good Housekeeping, 106
     (May 1938), 50-53, 154-163.

     Interviews with women writers, including
     Dorothy Canfield Fisher, Edna St. Vincent Millay,
     and Ellen Glasgow. Mainly descriptions of their
     gardens, with occasional mention of gardening and
     flowers in their writing.

405. Monroe, Harriet. "Literary Women and the Higher
     Education." Critic, 46 (Apr. 1905),
     313-318.

     Notes that few well-known women writing in
     English have held university degrees. Higher
     education may be too specialized for creative
     writers; advanced study of literature involves too
     much analysis and dissection.

406. Moore, Honor. "Polemic." Margins, No. 7
     (Aug.-Sept. 1973), 1-5.

     Poem advising women to write a new kind of
     poetry free of "the Male Approval Desire."

407. Rauch, Mabel Thompson. "For the Ladies." Writer,
     56 (June 1943), 179-180.

     Advice for women who want to write. A female
     writer's main problem is her household
     responsibilities; she can, however, plan her
     writing while doing routine household tasks or
     write about domestic subjects. Women should write
     "popular love stories." Realism, and especially
     any mention of sex, should be avoided because male
     editors do not like it.

408. Rayne, Martha L. "The Profession of Literature."
     What Can a Woman Do; or Her Position in the
     Business and Literary World. Petersburgh,
     N. Y.: Eagle Publishing Co., 1893. Pp. 25-33.

     Short survey of women's accomplishments in
     literature, advice to women on how to get
     published, where in their homes to write, etc.

409. Roberts, Ina Brevoort. "Woman and Author."
     Critic, 29 (Aug. 1901), 173-174.

     Melodramatic dialogue between Woman and Author
     (seen as male). Woman is an aspiring writer who
     seeks advice. Author tells her she must be willing
     to give up everything for her writing, including
     love; she becomes "white as death" as the Woman
     and the Writer inside her struggle, but the Writer
     wins out.

410. Shields, Sarah. "They Are Good at Two Jobs."
     Christian Science Monitor Weekly Magazine
     Section, Jan. 20, 1940, p. 6.

     Account of popular women writers who also
     keep house. Emphasis is on their writing methods:
     where they write, how they cope with domestic
     interruptions, etc.

411. Stern, Stella George. "My Lady of Literature."
Broadway Magazine, 17 (Jan. 1907), 477-484.

Informal biographical sketches of women
writers of the time. Includes Edith Wharton,
Alice Brown, Ellen Glasgow, and several less
well-known writers. (Received too late for
placement in biography section.)

412. "Two Letters from an Uncle to His Niece."
Southern Literary Messenger, 7 (May-June,
1841), 377-378.

The first letter is on "female poetry"
(the second is on corsets). Uncle tells Niece
there is nothing more dishonorable than a poetess.
"I look for a poetess to be slatternly in her dress
and person; a negligent and dirty housekeeper; an
inattentive, unsteady mother; a capricious or
peevish wife . . . ."

413. Walker, Gerald. "Typewriters in the Kitchen."
Cosmopolitan, 149 (Aug. 1960), 36-41.

Account of "writing housewives." Claims that
their number and success has greatly increased
over the past thirty years; women who want to earn
extra money or overcome inferiority feelings at
being "just a housewife" are motivated to write.
Quotes from interviews with several popular writers
who are also wives and mothers.

See also: 17, 28, 89, 145, 154, 156, 218, 250 (advice
and motives)

Poetry: 14, 16, 19, 30, 55, 60, 74, 96, 97, 108, 110,
116, 120, 124, 125, 127, 138, 143, 144, 149, 152,
159, 163, 167, 175, 180, 186, 189, 190, 208, 211,
214, 215, 217, 222, 230, 235, 236, 238, 240, 243,
247, 252, 256, 259, 260, 263, 267, 268, 269, 273,
281, 284, 291, 316, 321, 325, 334, 335, 339, 351,
355, 406

Drama: 32, 57, 95, 162, 172, 181, 183, 185, 192, 194,
197, 198, 199, 207, 213, 246, 249, 276, 286, 310,
315, 341, 361, 389

INDEX TO CRITICS AND EDITORS